# The Police Witness

## A Guide to Presenting Evidence in Court

# The author

Ronald Bartle, MA (Cantab),
Barrister-at-Law, and a
Metropolitan Stipendiary
Magistrate at Bow Street Court
from 1972 to 2000

# THE POLICE WITNESS

## A Guide to Presenting Evidence in Court

## Ronald Bartle

# The Police Witness
# A Guide to Presenting Evidence In Court

The first edition of this book was published by the
Police Review Publishing Co Ltd in 1984, entitled
The Police Officer in Court: A Guide to Presenting Evidence

Second edition 2002
ISBN: 1 903639 06 9

© Ronald Bartle 2002

Published by

the **NPB**
New Police
Bookshop

The New Police Bookshop
(Benson Publications)

Cover and illustrations by John Whittaker
The Cartoon Machine Co
Hoole Bridge, Chester

Printed and bound in Great Britain by
Antony Rowe Ltd, Eastbourne, East Sussex

Orders and customer services:
Brookland Mailing Services Unit 4, Parkway Trading Estate
St Werburghs Road, St Werburghs, Bristol  BS2 9PG
Tel 0117 9555 215  Fax 0117 9541 485
Email npb@brookland-mailing.co.uk

www.newpolicebookshop.co.uk

# Preface

*Order is heaven's first law*
Alexander Pope

*Before operating mouth, first engage brain*
Notice on the police room
in an East End Magistrates' Court

There are few more important functions for an individual in society than participating in the administration of justice. It is only within the context of law and order that other civilised activity can take place and the police officer, whose duty it is to combat crime and public vice and to maintain the peace, plays a crucial role. It is no exaggeration to say, although some of their fiercer critics might not agree, that the Police Force is the ultimate line of defence between order and chaos and between civilisation and barbarism.

The improvement of human society is a lamentably slow process – an unending battle between influences for good and for evil. The police officer, in being committed to the promotion of the former and the defeat of the latter is fulfilling a role of deep moral significance. It is precisely because that role upholds the authority of the law that the police are the guardians of individual liberty. The police officers' uniform is the badge and emblem of liberty under the law. His or her office is the heart, bone and marrow of civilisation and the human progress which takes place within it. This great responsibility must be discharged with integrity and efficiency.

The aim of this book is to help police officers perform their duty while acting as a witness in court. During the course of a career comprising 18 years at the Bar and 27 years as a Stipendiary Magistrate, I have had many opportunities to observe police officers in court and to follow and assess their evidence. I shall draw upon this experience and give examples of effective and ineffective practice in court which will help the police officer become a more confident and convincing witness. (This book does not comment on police duties prior to proceedings in court.)

There are two fundamental reasons why this aspect of police duties should be accorded great importance.

1   The administration of justice is so vital a task that all who take part in it should do so efficiently and well.

2   From the point of view of the police themselves, the result of a case depends very greatly upon the impression which witnesses make on the court.

Even in comparatively minor charges a considerable amount of work goes into the preparation of a case both on the part of the police and the Crown Prosecution Service. It can be frustrating and disheartening if a well-prepared prosecution fails due to an indifferent presentation of the case in court. When this occurs there may well be a temptation for the police to attribute the result of the case to other factors such as the guile of defending counsel; the skillful lying of the defendant or his or her witnesses; the gullibility of the bench or jury, or perhaps even the unfairness of the English trial process as seen from the point of view of the prosecution.

While these complaints may have some degree of justification it is sometimes the case that the poor showing of officers in the witness box, particularly under cross-examination, is equally to blame. This is no general criticism – officers frequently give their evidence very well. Yet sometimes police witnesses, particularly the younger and less experienced police witnesses tend to be hesitant, reticent and of poor audibility. Trainee police officers now receive instruction in presenting evidence in court. Ample time should always be devoted to this all-important topic, and with this in mind I offer what I hope will be useful guidance to my readers in the police service.

Throughout this book I have referred to police officers, magistrates, advocates and the accused in the male form. This is purely for ease and is not intended in any way to belittle or neglect the role of women in society and particularly in the valuable contribution they have made to the police force.

*Ronald Bartle*

# Table of Contents

The author                                    ii
Preface                                        v
List of Examples                              ix

## 1:  The Background Picture                  1

Statistics                                     1
The English Trial System                       3
The Alibi                                      4
The Case Against                               4
The Majority Verdict                           4
Evidence in Court                              5
Possible Changes to the Trial System           6

## 2:  Qualities of a Good Police Witness      9

First Impressions                              9
Presentation and Speech                       10
Impartiality                                  14
Terminology                                   16
The Police Officer's Notebook                 16
Basic Knowledge of Law and Evidence           19
Physical Force                                22
At the Police Station                         22
Top Ten Points for the Police Witness         24

## 3:  Role of the Defence Advocate           25

Aggressive Questioning                        27
Weak Questioning                              29
Irrelevant Questioning                        30
Complaints Against Police Officers            33
The Magistrates' Court                        33

## 4: Qualities of the Good Cross Examiner 37

| | |
|---|---|
| The Blanket Accusation | 37 |
| The 'Reasonable' Approach | 38 |
| The 'Alternative' Explanation | 46 |
| Identification | 49 |
| The ID Parade | 57 |
| Non-Compliance with PACE | 60 |
| Cross Examination in Particular Offences | 63 |

## 5: Tactics of the Cross Examiner 65

| | |
|---|---|
| 'Known' to the Police | 69 |
| Delaying Tactics | 74 |
| Expressing a View | 78 |

## 6: Points of Attack by the Defence 81

| | |
|---|---|
| Confessions | 81 |
| The Police and Criminal Evidence Act | 82 |
| Entrapment and the *Agent Provocateur* | 87 |
| Observation | 92 |
| Standing up to Cross Examination | 96 |

## 7: Bail 101

| | |
|---|---|
| Conclusion | 105 |
| Index | 107 |

# List of Examples

Throughout this book there are a number of examples of the type of situations Police Officers will encounter when appearing as a court witness. Some are from actual cases, while others are representative of what an officer can expect to face in particular instances. Some, you may 'recognise' while others you may yet have to face. However, all of them will help you increase the knowledge and skills you need to become an effective police witness in court.

| | | |
|---|---|---|
| 2.i | Hinting at previous bad character | 15 |
| 2.ii | Timing of entries in police notebook | 18 |
| 3.i | An aggressive defence advocate | 27 |
| 3.ii | A police witness responding aggressively | 29 |
| 3.iii | Weak questioning from the defence | 30 |
| 3.iv | Irrelevant questioning from the defence | 31 |
| 4.i | The blanket accusation - and denial | 37 |
| 4.ii | The 'sweetly reasonable' approach | 39 |
| 4.iii | Re-asserting the truth | 40 |
| 4.iv | A serious charge | 41 |
| 4.v | Questions the witness cannot answer | 42 |
| 4.vi | Arriving on scene after the event | 43 |
| 4.vii | The 'alternative' explanation (1) | 46 |
| 4.viii | The 'alternative' explanation (2) | 48 |
| 4.ix | Identification (1) | 50 |
| 4.x | Identification (2) | 53 |
| 4.xi | Identification (3) | 56 |
| 4.xii | ID parades | 57 |
| 4.xiii | Allegations of a 'plant' | 61 |
| 5.i | Yes/No questioning | 65 |
| 5.ii | Known to police – soliciting | 70 |
| 5.iii | Known to police – supplying drugs | 72 |
| 5.iv | Shifting the blame | 75 |
| 5.v | Assault charge | 78 |
| 5.vi | Adding comment (1) | 79 |
| 5.vii | Adding comment (2) | 79 |
| 5.viii | 'Putting in' good character | 80 |
| 6.i | Confessions (1) | 83 |
| 6.ii | Confessions (2) | 85 |
| 6.iii | Entrapment | 89 |
| 6.iv | Observation | 93 |
| 6.v | The value of frankness and brevity | 98 |

*Chapter One*

# The Background Picture

I t is evident at the time of writing, that there is much to tax the level of morale in the police service. In recent years many officers have left the service. Those remaining can be justified in feeling that their task has become a thankless one, in which they are constantly subjected to criticism and complaints. Reports such as those following the enquiries into the Hillsborough disaster and the murder of Stephen Lawrence, along with changes to police powers of 'stop and search', cannot but serve to exacerbate this trend. It appears to be an axiom of 'political correctness' that the police must shoulder some blame, whatever the general circumstances may be. The media likes to drag out the few 'bad apples' and relations between the police and the public suffer as a result. When such blows are aimed at police self-confidence, the community may well be the loser. A police force which is diminished in numbers, hesitant about searching for drugs and offensive weapons and increasingly subjected to assaults, both verbal and actual, is likely to suffer a decline in devotion to its work.

## Statistics

The difference between perception and reality is often a vital factor in determining the effectiveness of the police. Many people are extremely worried about crime and perceive the threat of crime to be very real. Statistics are therefore regularly compiled to help paint a clearer picture. However, Home Office figures on the current crime situation in England and Wales give a mixed view. In 1998/99 there were 5.1 million notifiable offences recorded by the police, a fall of 1.4% over 1997/8. Nevertheless the number of notifiable offences recorded by the police per 100,000 of the population rose from 5,200 in 1978 to 9,800 in 1998/9

Although the proportion of all offences in which firearms were reported to have been used remained at 0.3% in 1998/9, the number of firearms offences rose. Following falls in 1997, offences involving firearms, other than air weapons, rose by 6% in 1998/9 to 5,200.

Property crimes accounted for 84% of the total in 1998/9, amounting to 4.3 million. Violent crimes fell by 6%, burglary by 4% and vehicle crime by 2%. However, figures from the 1998 British Crime Survey suggest that less than one half of all offences are reported to the police and only a quarter are recorded.

The clear-up rate was 29% in 1998/9, little change from a year earlier, but still much lower than the high of 45% in the 1960s. The highest clear-up rate is for violent crime – more than 60%. The figures for sexual offences in 1998/9 rose by 2% and for robberies 6%. However, the 1998 British Crime Survey shows that for the sum of offences in categories that can be compared to those recorded by the police, the amount of crime actually committed is perhaps four times the number of crimes recorded by the police. There were three times more burglaries, three times as many woundings, eight times as many robberies and thefts from the person and four times as many thefts from vehicles. On a brighter note, 29 of the 43 police forces in England and Wales recorded fewer crimes in 1998/9 than in 1997/8. The largest falls were: Lancashire 10%; Avon and Somerset 9%; West Mercia 8%. Those with the largest rises were: City of London 18% and Greater Manchester 7%.

Looking at the conviction rate – the main point of interest in this book – 1998 figures reveal that the number of people committed for trial to the Crown Court was 73,000. Of these the number found guilty was 59,000. In Magistrates' Courts the proportion was 74% convictions and 26% dismissals. Of all the offences cleared up nationally by the police 5% resulted in cautions and 7% were not proceeded with.

The above figures reflect the crime situation nationally, but the latest statistics for London make grim reading. These show that the number of offences in the capital topped the million mark in the year ending May 2000 with increases in almost every category. Total crime was up 12.6%. Street crime has seen an increase of 36%; violent crime 19%; sex crime 13% and car crime 11%. The murder rate is up by 19%. These figures are largely the result of a much greater degree of criminal activity by young persons. As previously mentioned, powers of stop and search have been reduced and some research has shown that there is a link between the rise in street crime and a fall in the number of stop and searches. *The only four crimes to show reductions in detection rates in 1999 were those usually associated with stop and search activity by police, including possession of drugs, possession of an offensive weapon and handling stolen goods.*

This then is the general background scene: crime still at an alarmingly high rate; a burgeoning prison population; violence and sex offending and drug related crime at unacceptably high levels and a police service depleted by resignations and demoralised by criticism and complaints.

Yet, notwithstanding these discouraging factors, the police, aided by modern technology, have achieved some good results, especially in the realm of serious crime.

*It is vital that the good work done by police officers in bringing criminals to court is not undone by a poor showing in the witness box.*

## The English Trial System

There follows an examination of the criminal trial system as it stands in this country and how it affects police witnesses. Justice demands that an accusation of crime, always a serious matter, must be fully proved before any individual or group of people should be convicted and punished. The presumption of innocence must be kept sacrosanct. There is a body of opinion, however which feels the system is too heavily weighted in favour of the defence. One Commissioner of Police described to me a criminal trial as an "obstacle race" for the prosecution. Only when every hurdle has been cleared is a conviction possible.

It is believed by many that the adversarial system in our courts contains features which can be skillfully exploited by the defence to the disadvantage of the prosecution. Efforts have been made by recent governments to correct these anomalies and to redress the balance.

It must be accepted, however, that in the past many defendants were at a particular disadvantage, and more in need of the protection of the law than is the case today. In the nineteenth and much of the twentieth century there was rarely a solicitor sitting with a client advising him which questions should receive a response and which should not – this is now commonplace. Also, the introduction of the caution, by which a person under questioning by the police is warned about the prejudicial consequences of any statement he might make which could influence the trial, is aimed to help those with a lesser understanding of the law. *The absence of a caution, which amounts to a breach of the Police and Criminal Evidence Act (PACE), entitles the court to exclude the evidence concerned, but there is a discretion in the court to admit or rule out such evidence.*

## The Alibi

An example of redressing the balance is the requirement upon the defence to give notice of an alibi defence. In the past alibi witnesses could be sprung upon the prosecution without prior warning. It was difficult for their evidence to be effectively tested by cross-examination, and for the alibis to be checked involved an adjournment, and hence an interruption of the trial. Nowadays prior written notice of an alibi defence must be served on the prosecution before the trial commences, stating times, dates and places and a list of the witnesses with their details who will be called on the defendant's behalf to establish the alibi.

## The Case Against

It has always been a fundamental principle of our criminal law that a defendant must be fully apprised of the case against him, both in the particulars of the warrant of arrest and in the subsequent particulars of the charge and/or indictment. The prosecution, however, has remained in ignorance of the nature of the defence. This situation has now been amended by the obligation placed upon the defence to supply a written outline of the defence to be presented at trial to the prosecutor before commencement of the case – in all but summary matters.

It has long been an established principle of evidence that if a defendant fails to give evidence in his defence at the trial, only the judge may comment on this. Now the prosecution also may comment, within certain limits. It is also a basic precept of our law that the previous bad character of a defendant cannot be adduced in evidence.

*If a defendant, on instruction to his counsel, seeks to allege his or her own good character or attacks the character of Crown witnesses directly in cross-examination or by the manner of the conduct of the defence, his own previous convictions, with the leave of the court, can be put to him.*

## The Majority Verdict

Yet another innovation in recent years is the majority verdict. The requirement of a unanimous verdict meant that one juror could cause a perverse verdict to be the result, or could bring about a disagreement which necessitated a fresh trial. The verdict can be given on either ten to two or eleven to one basis, depending on the direction of the judge.

Thus we see that, if it is true that our trials are favourable to the defence, much has now been done to re-adjust the balance.

## Evidence in Court

The guilt or innocence of an accused person is decided upon solely by the evidence which is adduced in court. It is not determined by suspicion, or by the previous character of the defendant or by the speeches of counsel, however eloquent. Evidence which is regarded by the court as unreliable must be rejected, notwithstanding the fact that the witness who gives it may be entirely honest and perfectly genuine in his desire to assist in the furtherance of justice.

*An honest witness who is inaccurate is of no greater value than an accurate one who is dishonest.* This principle applies equally to the testimony of police officers as well as to lay men and women.

A policeman occupies no privileged position or special status in an English court. A judge may comment to the jury upon the expertise of a police officer, for example as a trained observer. He will remind the jury, however, that a policeman's uniform does not give him any greater right to be believed than the credibility which is accorded to any other occupant of the witness box. This having been said, it remains a fact that, strategically speaking, the police officer as a witness is in a different position from other deponents for three reasons:

1      The officer almost invariably gives evidence for the prosecution. The occasions on which police witnesses testify for the defence are very few indeed. This is because, although there is no property in a witness, the police are rarely able to assist the defendant.

2      Because it is the police who have investigated the alleged crime and caused the offender to be brought to court, they tend to be viewed as the bulwark and mainstay of the prosecution.

3      Police evidence, if accepted, is frequently damning to the defendant's hopes of acquittal.

For each of these reasons police officers are commonly singled out for special attention by the defending advocate. They are cross-examined with particular vigour and persistence since what they have to say usually constitutes a strong link in the chain of the prosecution evidence.

For example, consider a charge that has been made of interfering with a motor vehicle or stealing articles from within it. It may be comparatively simple for defending counsel to raise a doubt on the accuracy of the observation by witnesses, whether police or civilian. The actions of the accused may be open to an alternative explanation or of a nature which gives rise to doubt. The officer must anticipate, and doubtless will receive, very rough handling in cross- examination.

If however, the Crown calls a police witness to produce an alleged confession by the defendant, admitting his guilty intent, no amount of success in cross-examination of the earlier witnesses will avail the defendant – unless a doubt can be raised as to the genuineness of the purported confession statement. In these circumstances a police officer can expect to have his integrity and honesty impugned since this is an issue in which there can be no room for mistake.

There are some trials in which police testimony plays a very minor role and others where the whole of the evidence is only that of the police.

Examples of the latter are a burglary in which, as the result of a 'tip off' police are waiting in a nondescript vehicle; or again a charge of living on the earnings of prostitution. In these instances the totality of the evidence, both of observation and arrest, will be that of police witnesses. It is very important in such cases, from the point of view of the defence, that police witnesses are badly shaken in cross-examination. If this is not achieved the issue becomes a simple one of credibility as between the police and their witnesses on the one hand and the defendant and his on the other. If the defendant fares badly when cross-examined or his witnesses fail to impress the court the chances of an acquittal are substantially reduced.

## Possible Changes to the Trial System

Is the existing system unfair to the prosecution and are there further changes which could be made to correct this situation?

To begin with there is the matter of the oath. If everyone who told lies on oath in criminal cases were to be charged with perjury, there would be no court time to deal with anything else. And yet, on the basis of the conviction rate in contested cases in both the Crown and the Magistrates' Courts, it is clear that thousands of defendants and their supporting witnesses have attempted to evade the just consequences of their wrong-doing by telling the court a pack of lies.

*There is no doubt that many people tell lies after having gone into the witness box and sworn to tell the truth, the whole truth and nothing but the truth. I have heard a witness, by a slip of the tongue, swear to tell "anything but the truth", and so it proved to be! Perjury is one of the gravest crimes known to our law yet it is rarely invoked. Only in high profile cases in which the false evidence is the result of something approaching a conspiracy to concoct a bogus defence is a prosecution brought for this very serious offence.*

The prevailing view seems to be that a person will not be prosecuted for telling lies in his or her own defence. This is not a satisfactory situation. It reduces respect for the law and the courts and brings the oath itself into total contempt. Some people who take the oath in court treat it with appropriate respect, but a great many do not. This is particularly evident when they are persons of previous bad character while the majority of those who have no religious belief do not ask to take the affirmation – they simply say "C of E".

It may be more effective if the oath was abolished and replaced by a simple promise to tell the truth on pain of prosecution for perjury. Every witness in a criminal trial, whether called on behalf of the prosecution or the defence, should be made aware of the severe penalties for perjury before they give their evidence. That awareness should be confirmed in open court, perhaps by way of question and answer with the Bench.

Other issues which seem likely to be debated in the years ahead include the extent to which the trial system should be professionalised. Trial by jury has a long and much respected history in this country, and moves towards abolition would meet with very strong resistance. But there is always room for reform. Governmental proposals to limit the number of cases being committed for trial from Magistrates' Courts are an example of this. There is also an argument for allowing both prosecution and defence an unlimited number of challenges of the jury without cause being given. In the case of complicated fraud hearings, the jury should be replaced by a judge sitting alone or a judge with assessors with the agreement of both sides. Another question is the extent to which lay magistrates should be replaced by District Judges. Here again we have the delicate task of reforming an ancient and time-honoured institution which has worked reasonably well for five centuries. Nevertheless, the practice has grown in recent years of using Stipendiaries to deal with those cases which are regarded as too significant or too complex for the local Justices. With the coming of the new nationwide system of District Courts this tendency to professionalise the Magistrates' Courts will continue. There should always be, however, place in our judicial system for the Justices of the Peace.

*Chapter Two*

# Qualities Required of a Good Police Witness

Manner may seem to be a somewhat dated quality these days. But it is all-important in a witness in court. A relaxed and confident witness makes a good impression straight away. The court will closely scrutinise the person giving evidence, looking for those signs of insecurity which undermine the effectiveness of the evidence being given. A 'shifty' manner, licking the lips and hesitant delivery are symptoms of something less than the integrity exemplified by a firm gaze and a strong voice.

A relaxed witness is also a confident one, but these attributes are not innate - they can be acquired - and the young PC in particular must consciously and deliberately cultivate them. An excellent way to develop this quality is to simulate it before one actually possesses it. The classic advice to inexperienced speakers has always been to "get up, speak up and shut up". This is not at all bad advice, but I will aim in this chapter to demonstrate how to build on this so that each aspect of being an effective witness becomes second nature.

## First Impressions

The impression made by a witness commences from the moment he or she enters the witness box and takes the oath or affirmation. It is a very bad start if the court, at that early stage, has to comment: "Officer, you will have to speak louder than that if your evidence is to be heard".

Notwithstanding my earlier comments in the previous chapter, the oath remains a solemn promise to tell the truth and the procedure of making that promise must be treated very seriously. If the oath is taken in a casual or off-hand manner it may well convey the impression to the court that the witness has an equally indifferent attitude towards the truth. The same effect may be given if the words are gabbled off at great speed. Police witnesses are especially in danger of doing this due to their great familiarity with the procedure. This may cause the magistrate or judge to comment: "Now officer, start again and this time go more slowly". Such an intervention may be embarrassing for the witness and is a poor beginning to his or her evidence.

A good visual presence - which is much more than simply having smart attire - is important because it carries with it an air of authority which a poor appearance lacks. The perfunctory manner, the downcast eye, the hands spread across the witness box like a man ordering a pint of beer at his 'local' combine to create an inert and apathetic picture. "Look alert you lot" is the advice given on the parade ground by the Sergeant Major, and it is a sound precept in court also. *Stand up straight and look towards the bench.* This has the double merit of showing courtesy and producing greater audibility.

In a Crown Court the evidence should be directed towards the jury during the trial, and to the judge after conviction or when the plea has been one of guilty and you have been called to deal with any aspects of the antecedents. Thus you make it plain that you are there to assist the court and not for the benefit of counsel.

*The root of confidence in the witness box is to be well prepared in what you are going to say.*

In strict law a police officer enjoys no superior position in the witness box to any other deponent. But as all who know life are well aware that principle and practice frequently diverge. Police officers, because of their training and expertise, are *expected* to be better witnesses than lay people. Their uniform adds the weight of impartiality to their evidence.

## Presentation and Speech

The mode of presentation of evidence is almost as important as the content, and foremost in presentation is audibility. I have touched upon this point already, *but it cannot be too strongly emphasised*. A strong voice commands respect in court for two reasons:

1    It greatly eases the task of the court if it is unnecessary to strain the ears trying to hear what is being said.

2    A powerful voice is authoritative and carries conviction. A lying witness, unless he is a consummate actor, rarely raises his voice.

*Vocal clarity has the ring of integrity and sincerity.*

Generally speaking police witnesses do not offend greatly in this respect. Regretfully, however, the performance of some of the younger officers in this regard is sometimes very poor. *What is it that appears to make some people fearful of the sound of their own voices?* A young officer whose words are plain to hear in the office canteen may lower his voice to a reverential murmur in court. It is fair to say that lay witnesses offend more frequently in this respect, but they, unlike police, receive no training for the task.

*One cannot help recalling the policeman of yesteryear who frequently made his appearance in the humourous novels and plays of the 1930s and was immortalised in the television series Dixon of Dock Green. His portly figure filled the witness box, and from his close-cropped head surmounting the buttoned up tunic there emerged a voice of stentorian power which reassured good citizens of the impregnability of the law while at the same time striking fear into the hearts of wrongdoers. No doubt our police of today are every bit as formidable as their forebears. It is very important that they are seen to be so in court.*

It is worth noting that members of the judiciary, and a large number of the jury, are middle-aged. It is a commonly known fact that in middle life the physical faculties decline, and this includes acuteness of hearing. Unfortunately many people, through pride or unawareness of change in themselves, refuse to accept this fact. They prefer the strain of endeavouring to hear, even at the risk of missing something important in the evidence, rather than use one of the extremely effective and entirely inconspicuous hearing aids now available. This is due to a widely held but wholly illogical view that spectacles, which assist the eyesight, are not ageing, but aids to hearing are.

*The tale is told of a judge who sat many years ago in a County Court. He used a hearing aid of an early variety. It resembled a radio and the apparatus included headphones worn by the judge. On a social occasion he was asked "Don't you find that having to use that contraption is an impediment to your work?" "On the contrary" replied the judge smiling "I find it an advantage". "An advantage?" he was asked with surprise. "Yes," said the judge "whenever I find myself getting bored I can switch off without anyone knowing". No modern member of the bench need face the difficulties suffered by the judge in this particular story.*

The problem of audibility becomes more acute if a witness fails to look up as well as speak up. The best voice becomes useless if remarks are addressed to the desk below and not towards the hearer. For police witnesses, who may be reading from documents this is especially important. Examples occur when an officer is referring to his notebook or reading the confession of a defendant. *Hold the document well up and read the contents in a loud voice.*

Apart from the inherent quality of clear, resonant speech, poor diction is particularly disastrous in court because of the conditions which prevail there. In many courts, particularly older ones, acoustics are poor and efforts to improve them whether by modern building innovations or the installation of electronic amplifying equipment frequently seem to achieve little improvement. It must be appreciated that in court a witness must speak more loudly, much more loudly, than in ordinary conversation. It is also necessary to speak more forcefully. Witnesses sometimes lower their voices in court because of a sense of awe at their surroundings. This is wholly misguided. Nothing is more irritating to a judge or magistrate than having continually to interrupt a witness to tell him or her to speak up. It dislocates the proceedings and detracts from that air of dignity which should at all times pervade a court of law.

Diction is as important as volubility. There is nothing whatever wrong with a 'regional' accent provided the words are spoken clearly and distinctly.

*It is said that Demosthenes, the great Greek orator, achieved his superb articulation by filling his mouth with pebbles and declaiming while running up hill. It might be a little drastic to suggest that this method be adopted at police training schools, but the point should not be ignored.*

Among other common faults, one is to speak too quickly. In a Magistrates' Court the clerk has to take a note of the evidence. Time and again in a trial the clerk has to request police officers and other witnesses to speak more slowly, and time and again the offence is repeated. The solution could not be simpler. Watch the clerk's pen. Most court clerks have the ability to record evidence in longhand at almost conversational speed. Only when the witness is speaking too quickly is the clerk in a difficulty. Time is lost if the unfortunate clerk has continually to plead for breathing space.This applies also in a Crown Court, where it is the judge who takes note of the evidence. He may become very irate with a witness who offends in this way.

## Impartiality

However impressive a witness he may be, a police officer in the box should always give an impression of fundamental impartiality. It is the task of the police to bring offenders to book, but only those against whom adequate evidence exists can be properly convicted. *A policeman must not allow himself to become emotionally involved with his work.* If he does he will be too preoccupied with the outcome of a case. This is very human and understandable, but is also dangerous. It is not the approach of the true professional.

Those who see themselves as engaged in a crusade against crime should remember that crime has been in the world since the dawn of the human race. There are no grounds for supposing human nature will ever be suppressed. The best that society in each generation can achieve is to control and contain the worst excesses. To say this is to counsel reality, not complacency. I have known instances of police officers being profoundly depressed when a defendant, of whose guilt they had no doubt, has been acquitted. This is understandable. They feel that a great deal of hard work has gone for nothing, and that in addition a miscarriage of justice has occurred. Such feelings should be suppressed - at least temporarily.

*It is unattractive to see police officers leaving court looking openly disgruntled at the result of a case. These emotions are better reserved for the canteen when views regarding the judicial capacity of members of the bench or jury can be freely expressed, and no doubt frequently are.*

Impartiality requires that a police officer is scrupulously fair in the way he gives his evidence. There must be no show of hostility towards defending counsel, even when the latter is cross-examining with some vigour.

Everyone in court has a task to perform in the administration of justice. A criminal trial is a drama in which the role of each of the principal actors may bring him into conflict with one of the others. Counsel may clash with the judge, defending counsel may come into conflict with prosecuting counsel and sparks may fly between advocates and witnesses. This element of conflict in a trial is a necessary part of the process by which evidence is tested and weighed.

Even when sorely tried by the defence, an officer must *never* seek to score a point by improper or prejudicial observations. I refer here to a hint of the previous bad character of the accused or of the fact that at the time of the alleged offence he was under investigation for other matters.

**Example 2.i   Hinting at previous bad character**

Q:   Are you sure officer, that the man you arrested in Green Park was the same person you had seen 20 minutes earlier tampering with a Rolls Royce car in Berkeley Square?

A:   *I am quite sure.*

Q:   How can you be so certain?

A:   *Your client was known to me.*

Q:   Do you mean that you had seen him on an earlier occasion in the Berkeley Square area?

A:   *Not in the Berkeley Square area.*

Q:   You mean you had seen him before that day?

A:   *I mean that I had had dealings with him on other occasions.*

Q:   But not in connection with motor vehicles?

A:   *No. Not in connection with motor vehicles.*

In this example the officer is practically stating the accused person has a criminal record. The line of cross-examination may appear to invite it, but it should be avoided. The officer should confine himself to saying that he knew the defendant by sight, however ambiguous that may sound.

*A police officer has many opportunities for showing fairness and generosity after conviction or when the defendant pleads guilty. If the defendant is unrepresented a few words in mitigation do not go amiss, for example that the defendant has been helpful to the police in their enquiries. If the accused is a known informer very special care has to be taken. Normally the judge or magistrate will be informed of this fact privately before the proceedings commence. There are obvious reasons why it should not be mentioned in open court. If the defendant has shown genuine remorse or concern for the distress he has brought upon his family these factors are worthy of mention. There is a noble tradition in the British police that when a defendant makes a clean breast of things and throws himself upon the mercy of the court, the police, if there is something good to be said for him, will say it.*

## Terminology

When giving evidence terminology is important. Do not use abbreviations. These are all too common and personally I wince whenever I hear them. For example 'haughty' should describe an attitude of false pride and not a form requiring a motorist to produce his driving documents. Worse still is the description given to the number of a motor vehicle such as "Charlie, Mike, Oscar, Victor" etc. An officer using this form of verbiage sounds more like a vicar at a christening than a constable in court.

When giving dates name the day and month rather than speaking of the "first of the fifth". Never refer to a case or an investigation as a 'job' and always refer to a charge properly and not as 'TDA' or 'GBH'. Any kind of informality detracts from the dignity of the court. This is one area where certain modern trends have to be resisted.

## The Police Officer's Notebook

It is remarkable how uncomfortable and self-conscious some officers are when referring to their notebook. They glance at it surreptitiously as though it were a pornographic photograph. Halsbury's Laws of England states: *"A witness is permitted to refresh his memory in the course of his evidence by reference to documents or memoranda. The document or memorandum must have been made either at the time of the events described in it or so shortly afterwards that the facts were fresh in the witness' memory. It need not have been made by the witness personally, but if it was not made by him it must have been checked by him while the facts were fresh in his memory".*

Professor Cross, the great authority on evidence, sets out the law on this subject very clearly: *"Although a witness may not give his evidence to the court by reciting a prepared statement such as his proof of evidence, he is allowed to refer to a document in order to refresh his memory, provided certain conditions are fulfilled. The document must have been made substantially at*

*the same time as the occurrence of the events to which the witness is required*
*to depose; it must have been made or read over by, or under the supervision of,*
*the witness; it must be produced to the court or opposite party on demand, and*
*in one class of case (when the witness cannot speak from his own recollection*
*alone) the document must be the original".*

After giving his name and rank the officer should ask leave of the court
to refer to his notebook. This is an act of courtesy. He should then inform
the Bench of the period of time which elapsed between the events leading up to arrest and the making of the note. A definite time should be
given, even if only approximate. It is not satisfactory to say "shortly after
arrest" or "as soon as I got back to the station".

It is not essential that an officer should be able to remember the facts
irrespective of his note, nor is he or she bound to remember what has
been recorded. Consequently the familiar question "Have you any recollection of the events apart from your note?" can be answered with a
confident "No".

A common query from the defence is: "When did you make your
note?" The question of whether a note is to be regarded as contempora-
neous is a matter of fact and degree. The correct test is that the document
must have been written either at the time of the transaction or so shortly
afterwards that the facts were still fresh in the memory of the witness at
the time of making. It is only on rare occasions that an officer's notebook
is likely to be excluded by the court on these grounds, since a period as
long as a fortnight has been considered acceptable. Intervals of several
weeks or months clearly cannot qualify. One officer may refresh his
memory from the notebook of another provided that he read that other's
note and agreed it as correct within the admissible time limit. In such a
situation he would be well advised to sign it at the time of recording.

There is nothing whatever objectionable about two officers compiling
their notes after mutual consultation - although Advocates, decade after
decade suggest that there is. If the notebook has gone missing the officer
may refresh his memory from a written statement based upon the note,
provided that the note itself passes the above test.

Police witnesses must expect lengthy, sometimes almost interminable
cross-examination on the contents of their notes. In virtually hopeless
cases there is often little that defending counsel can do save attack the
'verbals'. The type of questions put are likely to relate to the following
matters:

1       When the notes were made. If not at the time why not?

2.      Whether they were made in conjunction with another officer.

3       If they were made as in (2) what passed between the officers.

4       Whether or not the notes are a full and complete record of what occurred or what was said.

5       Were the notes completed at one 'sitting' or several?

6       If at several, has a time been recorded for each separate portion?

The officer who is thoroughly versed in the evidence he will give and familiar with the rules of evidence relating to notes need have nothing to fear from vigorous cross-examination.

**Example 2.ii     Timing of entries in the notebook**

Q:      Were your notes made contemporaneously or later on?

A:      *They were made later.*

Q:      How much later?

A:      *Two hours after the time of the defendant's arrest.*

Q:      Was your memory clear after a lapse of two hours?

A:      *Perfectly clear.*

Q:      Can you recall the words I used when I was addressing their worships about an hour ago? *(A familiar forensic stratagem).*

A:      *No I cannot.*

Q:      Why is that? You can remember what my client said after two hours, but not what I said after only one.

A:      *Because I was not arresting you for a criminal offence when your words were spoken and had no particular reason to commit them to memory.*

Q:      Are you telling the court that you faithfully and accurately recorded every word spoken by the defendant two hours after the conversation?

A:      *No. I am saying that I accurately recorded whatever was material to the charge.*

Q:      Where was the defendant when you and your fellow officer made up your notes?

A:      *At the police station.*

Q:      Did you give my client an opportunity of reading and approving your note as a correct account of what he had said to you?

A:      *I did.*

Q:      Were your notes completed all in one sitting?

A:      *No. Some were made on my arrival at the police station and the remainder were completed about an hour after that.*

Q:      Why the lapse of time between the two sets of notes?

A:      *I was interrupted by having to attend another matter.*

Q:      In completing the notes did you have to rely on your colleague's recollection?

A:      *No. My own memory was still clear.*

Q:      Have you entered in your book the time of making each portion of the notes?

A:      *I have.*

Q:      Are you relying on the contents of your notebook alone as adequate evidence on which to convict my client? *(Another favourite forensic stratagem.)*

A:      *That is for the court, and not for me to decide.*

## Basic Knowledge of Law and Evidence

It is not my intention to examine in detail the law of evidence and criminal procedure so far as it impinges upon the every day work of the police. These matters are fully covered by instruction in police training schools and in the various manuals available to trainee officers. I do however wish to emphasise, from the point of view of effective evidence in court, how vitally important it is to have a good working knowledge of these matters. This is because defending advocates will seize any opportunity that may arise to attack and exploit any misuse of or ignorance about the statutory powers of the police concerning a range of issues including:

*   Stop and search.
*   Search of premises.
*   Arrest with or without warrant.
*   The use of force when carrying out an arrest.
*   Interviews both at time of arrest and later at the police station.
*   Administering of a caution before the statement is taken down.
*   The correct procedure in the case of youthful and mentally retarded persons in custody.

For this reason the legislation with which an officer must be fully versed includes the *Police and Criminal Evidence Act 1984* and the *Codes of Practice and the Criminal Justice and Public Order Act 1994.*

Police officers must be aware that the defence counsel, if he knows his job well, is ever vigilant to find grounds for claiming the prosecution case has been vitiated by a technicality or by reason of which the court can be influenced to find a doubt. For example in a case stemming from a stop and search incident, it may be suggested in cross-examination that the officer did not have reasonable grounds to suspect that the defendant had upon his person incriminating items. The officer must be very clear indeed what the actions of the defendant or the prevailing circumstances at the time were which gave rise to that reasonable suspicion. The inference may well be that the defendant was 'picked on' for reasons of colour or disreputable appearance.

Similarly, with search of premises the police witness must be fully conversant with police powers and make sure that they have been strictly complied with. Juries, whose members tend to be younger and of more varied social and ethnic background than in previous times, are especially sensitive to any heavy-handedness or 'cutting of corners' in police procedure. If this is true of arrest and search it is doubly so where the use of force is concerned.

The police witness must have a good working knowledge of the rules of evidence. (This again is for the purpose of emphasis, because these things are the subject of instruction at police training school.) Generally speaking, admissibility of the prosecution evidence is the responsibility of the Crown Advocate, normally a member of the Crown Prosecution Service. The questions put in examination-in-chief must, and generally will, elicit answers which do not infringe the basic rules of evidence. However, under cross-examination it may sometimes happen that the police witness does say something which contravenes the rules. One obvious example is the rule against hearsay. A statement made in interview with one defendant which involves another must not be put into evidence unless it is made in the presence of that other. This is because the other person should have an opportunity of accepting or rejecting something which might be to his or her prejudice at the trial. A further point concerns the caution. A caution need not be given while the questions being put to a suspect merely consist of an enquiry into whether or not an offence has been committed. But once it is clear to the investigating officer that a crime has occurred, and a decision has been made to charge the suspect, a caution must be administered. *If it is not given this is a clear breach of PACE.* Even though the court still has a discretion to admit the evidence if its evidential value outweighs its prejudicial effect, officers should endeavour to abide strictly by the PACE rules. When a caution has not been given the police witness must be prepared to provide the court with a careful explanation for the failure to do so.

Examination-in-chief and cross-examination is discussed in more detail later in this book, however. I refer to this subject briefly at this point in the context of the qualities required to make a good police witness. The purpose of the cross-examiner is to undermine the credibility of a witness. This can rarely be done by dramatic confrontational methods which are more appropriate to fictional rather than actual criminal trials. Occasionally the cross-examiner has the stroke of luck which enables him to produce a document or some other item of evidence which exposes the testimony of the witness as patently untrue. This, however, is comparatively rare. The task of cross-examination is normally much more uphill than that, as barristers and solicitors know only too well. The golden rule under questioning by the defence is to remain calm and to deal with the questions thoughtfully and with an economical use of language. *However convinced you may be of the defendant's guilt do not let this become apparent in the way questions are answered.* A hostile attitude towards the defence is almost always counterproductive.

Examination-in-chief is ostensibly a much easier experience for a witness in that the advocate is a friend and not a foe. Nevertheless, it has its pitfalls. In the Magistrates' Courts particularly, counsel is frequently of the more junior and less experienced type and sometimes fails to guide and control its own witnesses in the correct manner. In my experience on the Bench, a prosecuting advocate would sometimes remain seated and leave the police witness to tell the whole 'story'. This is a most improper and thoroughly lazy way to call a witness. Even when examination-in-chief is more competently conducted the questions have to be carefully put and competently answered. Again, as a general principle, brevity and clarity are the golden rules. Never get into a 'discussion' with the advocate. Never base your answer on a presumption or conclusion. If you are unable to answer the question simply say so. I shall give examples of this a little later on.

Sometimes there will be interventions by the court. These will normally be to elicit or clarify matters of detail. A witness must always be prepared for interventions by the court.These are generally to clarify matters of uncertainty. It is wrong and contrary to the traditions of British justice for judges and magistrates to cross-examine a witness. Courtesy must be shown to the Bench in dealing with any such questions and care taken to use the correct terms of address: "Your worship" to lay justices, "Sir" or "Madam" to a stipendiary and "Your honour" to a circuit judge.

## Physical Force

Sometimes the police have no option but to exercise a considerable degree of force when a person who is being restrained is violently resisting arrest. It is not easy, in the heat of the moment, to be sure exactly how much force is necessary. It is especially difficult to judge when use of the truncheon is justified. But whatever the exact nature of the physical force used, it will almost certainly be a subject of debate in court. The police witness must be scrupulous in being able to explain and justify such methods.

## At the Police Station

Events at the police station are another area of investigation by the defence in a criminal trial. Frequently advocates are instructed by their clients that they have been maltreated while in custody, either because they have been subjected to some form of brutality or because they have been induced to make a confession by improper promises. A common allegation is that officers have suggested that they will be released on bail provided they 'come clean' and admit to the offence. In addition, it may be alleged that their statement has been taken without the requirements of PACE being observed. The grounds on which the validity of a statement may be challenged are numerous. Another frequent objection is that comments which are damaging to the accused were made at the prompting of the officer, or even invented by him, or that the defendant, being foreign, did not understand what was being put to him. All these are points for which the police witness must be prepared.

*The fact that a complaint has been made against police is, of course, no evidence whatever that undue force has been used, but there are occasionally examples, some of which came before me when I was on the Bench, of police officers who, because of severe provocation, failed to exercise that degree of control which is a crucial element of police work. Just one such case can do untold harm to the good name of the police service.*

## Top Ten Points for the Police Witness

To conclude this chapter outlined below is a summary of the 10 main principles of being an effective witness.

1    Be confident and look confident. This can be achieved by having thoroughly in mind the matters about which you are going to give your evidence.

2    From the moment of taking the oath speak in a loud, clear voice.

3    Think carefully before answering questions but when you do so reply in a straight forward and simple manner, using the utmost economy of words. Avoid expanding upon your initial answer.

4    Be frank. If you cannot remember something say so. Never agree with any proposition put to you in cross-examination unless you are able to do so with truth and accuracy.

5    Do not express an opinion, although invited to do so by counsel.

6    Never feel or display embarrassment about the use of your note-book (see previous chapter).   .

7    Always exercise complete self-control in the witness box, even when under cross-examination which involves an attack upon your professional integrity. Remember that the allegations originate from the defendant and not from counsel.

8    Adhere unswervingly to the facts as you know them. Never give an answer based upon a conclusion which you have drawn from those facts. Never be charmed into compromise or bullied into recantation.

9    Do not be preoccupied with the outcome of the case. Play your part in the impartial administration of justice by doing your work, in court and out of it, efficiently and effectively.

10   Give vent to any feelings you may have about the verdict or sentence in the police canteen - not in court.

*Chapter Three*

# The Role of the Defence Advocate

This chapter examines the profession of advocate and its nature and purpose. It is important that the police witness, perhaps on the principle of 'know thine enemy' should understand what the defending barrister or solicitor is trying to achieve and the methods which may be employed in pursuit of that end. It must be borne in mind, however, that the abler and more experienced counsel usually appears in the higher courts. Solicitors have the right of audience in the Crown Court, and although advocacy is the speciality of the Bar, in my experience some of the solicitor advocates who practice regularly in the Magistrates' Court have considerable ability in this field.

In most contested criminal cases the defence has an uphill task. And advocate is only too aware of this. It is possible that the majority of those who protest their innocence in court are guilty as charged. The statistics showing the conviction rates and the numbers of those committed for trial who subsequently plead guilty would seem to support this view, most innocent people arrested having already been released without charge.

There is a prevailing idea that a defendant's chances of acquittal are greater before a jury than in a Magistrates' Court. Counsel feel that they have more room for manoeuvre in a Crown Court than in front of a magistrate or magistrates. If there are powerful mitigating circumstances it may be thought by the defence advocate that, notwithstanding the state of the evidence, a favourable verdict can be extracted from a jury. In many contested cases the evidence for the Crown is such that the chances of actually convincing the court of the defendant's innocence are slim indeed. Therefore counsel must rely on the principle that if there is a reasonable doubt the defendant is entitled to the benefit of it. However, a Stipendiary Magistrate, being a professional lawyer, may well be a better judge of what amounts to 'reasonable' in this context than a member of a jury. The essence of defending in a criminal trial is to minimise points favourable to the prosecution and maximise those which assist the defence. But some points have far more substance than others and it is not always easy for a jury, especially on their first few cases, to distinguish between those aspects of the evidence which are significant and those which are not. For example the case for the Crown may rest in part on identification and in part on scientific evidence (e.g. DNA or finger-prints). Since the scientific evidence is difficult to argue with, the defence may concentrate on discrediting the identification. Should it succeed in this latter, the suggestion may then be made that notwithstanding the scientific experts there has to be an overall doubt. It should be said, in fairness to the defence, that the prosecutor will adopt such tactics as are favourable to his side of the case.

*The profession of advocate has sometimes been stigmatised as morally dubious. The perennial question is: how can you defend someone whom you know to be guilty? The standard answer to this question is that judge-ment as to guilt or innocence is for the jury, not for counsel, and that in any event any person accused of crime is entitled to say: "You prove it". Very few people would be able efficiently to defend themselves in court, and since the prosecution is represented by an expert they too, in all equity and justice, should be defended by an expert in the same profession.*

There are ethical principles which govern the profession of both barris-ters and solicitors as advocates.There is no doubt many lawyers defend clients on a plea of not guilty while having a private doubt about their guilt. One cannot close one's mind to the obvious. Nevertheless it is their duty to put their client's account, however improbable, before the court and to do so to the best of their ability. *What must not be done is to delib-erately mislead the court.* If, during interview, the defendant actually admits guilt or makes a comment which is only consistent with guilt the lawyer must advise his client to plead guilty. If this advice is not accepted counsel must withdraw from the case.

Any profession is prey to corruption. That is why the division of the legal profession in this country into the Bar and Solicitors is so valuable, especially in the field of crime. Close proximity between criminal defen-dants and the advocate can lead to dangers for the latter. An unhealthy familiarity can develop which may undermine ethical standards. In the case of members of the Bar, the disciplinary bodies are the Bar Council and the Benchers of the offender's Inn of Court. For solicitors it is the disciplinary committee of The Law Society.

The position with regard to the duty of disclosure of previous convic-tions is that if these are not known to prosecuting counsel there is no obligation on the part of the defence to reveal them. On the other hand no suggestion or hint must be made indicating that the defendant is a person of good character. Also, an attack by the defence lawyer upon the character of prosecution witnesses may, at the discretion of the judge, entitle the prosecution to cross-examine the defendant on this same subject.

Advocates differ greatly in both style and ability. Poor advocates are much more easily handled by a witness than good ones. Since the art of cross-examination is a difficult one which takes time and experience to master, the less skilled tend to be the younger members of the profession, but not always so. Some lawyers simply never master this aspect of their work.

The next section of this chapter deals with the hallmarks of poor cross-examination which the police witness will no doubt encounter from time to time.

## Aggressive Questioning

There is a saying that good cross-examining is not examining crossly. Aggressive questioning of a witness is nearly always a sign of either incompetence or inexperience on the part of counsel. A calm and digni-fied demeanour on the part of the police witness when assailed in this manner is the correct course. An advocate who lacks the subtlety and the finesse, and sometimes it must be said the basic talent for the job, will try to compensate by angry and hostile questioning. When the approach bears no fruit the advocate becomes frustrated and hence even more belligerent. The point may be reached when the prosecuting counsel, or even the judge, should intervene. *What the police witness must not do is to reply in kind.*

**Example 3.i    An aggressive defence advocate**

Q:      How long have you been in the force officer?

A:      *I have been a member of the police service for 9 years.*

Q:      You have taken the oath in this case?

A:      *I have.*

Q:      That obliges you to tell the truth?

A:      *It does. I have told the truth.*

Q:      The defendant will say that you are making this up.

[This is not a proper question in any event since the defence, at this stage, does not know for certain what the defendant is going to say in evidence. A more correct way of putting the question would be:

"If the defendant were to say ... what would be your answer?"]

A:      *I am telling the truth.*

Q:      You say that you saw him 'dipping'?

A:      *I saw him putting his hand into the young lady's holdall.*

Q:      How long had you been watching him when this happened?

A:      *About 10 minutes*

Q:      And he did nothing wrong?

A:      *He was behaving suspiciously.*

Q:      That is a typical police expression?

A:      *He was hanging about on the pavement looking at women's handbags.*

Q:      Is that a crime?

A:      *It gave rise to reasonable suspicion.*

Q:      Suspicion of what?

A:      *Suspicion that he might steal or attempt to steal a bag or its contents.*

Q:      That is pure prejudice is it not officer?

A:      *It is not.*

Q:      He is of scruffy appearance?

A:      *You could say that.*

Q:      And that is why you arrested him?

A:      *It is not.*

Q:      Sheer prejudice on your part?

A:      *It is not.*

Q:      Picking people up on this charge is an easy number for the police?

A:      *I decline to answer a comment like that.*

A good witness possesses quiet confidence and dignity without any hint of anger or acrimony. Altercations of the following kind, which I have experienced, must be avoided:

### Example 3.ii    A police witness responding aggressively

Q:     Officer, is it not right that you called my client a villain who would strangle his own grandmother for a pound?

A:     *No sir. I don't think even your client would go to those lengths.*

Q:     Is it not my client's good fortune to be a man of good character?

A:     *Your client is indeed fortunate not to have any previous convictions recorded against him.*

*It is natural, when under cross-examination by an advocate whose manner is somewhat hectoring, to feel provoked. The same reaction may be felt when the questions relate to allegations of misconduct such as an alleged assault by police on the defendant, or improper pressure to obtain a confession statement. But signs of anger will make you appear motivated and far from impartial. A police witness must be cool 'under fire'.*

## Weak questioning

Another form of poor cross-examination but one which is easy for the witness to meet is mere confrontation. This is punctuated by such terms as "I put it to you" or "I suggest" or even more ineffectually "I have to suggest to you". This puts the witness in the position of simply having to disagree with the questioner.

**Example 3.iii    Weak questioning**

Q:     I have to suggest to you officer, on the defendant's behalf, that what you call resisting arrest was no more than self-defence against your excessively rough tactics?

A:     *I did not adopt rough tactics when arresting the defendant.*

Q:     Are you quite sure about that?

       [A useless question since a witness always repeats that they are sure.]

A:     *I am perfectly sure.*

Q:     I put it to you that you seized the defendant around the neck causing him great pain?

A:     *No.*

Q:     You used excessive force?

A:     *I used reasonable force to restrain him from struggling.*

Q:     I suggest you used more force than was necessary?

A:     *I did not.*

Q:     I have to put it to you on behalf of my client that he never resisted arrest.

A:     *He did.*

This kind of blank confrontation, although it puts the defence case, is of no value whatever in assisting the court to decide where the truth lies. Yet the police witness will frequently encounter it.

Just as a poor speaker will get down thinking he has put up an impressive performance so an incompetent cross-examiner, who generates more heat than light, often thinks that bullying, badgering tactics help his case. Nothing could be further from the truth. Frequently it alienates the court and rarely achieves any progress with the witness.

## Irrelevant questioning

A third type of ineffectual questioning which the police witness will encounter in court is concentration on the irrelevant. Nothing is more frustrating to a court than to have to listen to an endless interrogation of a witness on matters which are not of the essence of the issues in the case. If any advocate is guilty of this defect it is a clear sign that he or she does not possess the basic skills of the job.

**Example 3.iv    Irrelevant questioning**

Q:    The police have prosecuted my client under the Public Order Act?

A:    *The Crown Prosecution Service brings the prosecution. The police charged him with that office.*

Q:    Don't split hairs officer. That is the offence charged?

A:    *I am not splitting hairs sir, merely stating the position. That is the offence charged under Section Five of the Public Order Act.*

Q:    You claim to have seen this defendant throw a bottle at police lines?

A:    *That is what he did.*

Q:    This was a 'demo' - with a big attendance?

A:    *There were many people at the demonstration.*

Q:    In Trafalgar Square?

A:    *Yes.*

Q:    About how many?

A:    *I cannot say how many.*

Q:    Can you make a guess officer?

A:    *I would say several hundred.*

Q:    It was a noisy demonstration?

A:    *Yes.*

Q:    The demonstration was against the fur trade?

A:    *Yes.*

Up to this point it could be said that the advocate is legitimately 'setting the scene'. Nevertheless, if he continues on this line of questioning the court may soon get restive over the fact that the nub of the case has still not been reached - namely whether a bottle was thrown, and if so whether or not it was the defendant who threw it.

Q:      The demonstrators clearly had strong feelings about it?

A:      *Yes.*

Q:      There were banners denouncing the fur trade?

A:      *There were.*

Q:      Where there many banners?

A:      *Quite a lot.*

Q:      What do you mean by quite a lot - about how many?

A:      *I would say about 20 or 30.*

Q:      Can't you be more specific officer?

A:      *Between 20 and 30.*

Q:      They were obviously sincere in their views?

A:      *I presume so.*

Q:      It was plain that the defendant was sincere?

A:      *I cannot answer for the defendant.*

Q:      He gave that impression after his arrest?

A:      *Yes. He gave that impression.*

Counsel is now getting onto matters which may relate to mitigation, but which have no relevance to the central issue in the charge. There is little that the police witness can do save reply to the questions. Normally it is for the court or prosecuting counsel to intervene. The police witness will sometimes have to cope with questions which are not proper questions at all but mere comment, and often offensive comment at that.

**Examples:**

*   You understand officer that you are on oath.
*   How long have you been in the force?
*   You arrested the defendant because of his appearance.
*   You arrested this man because of his colour.
*   The police are always picking up women in this area.
*   You have a low view of prostitutes.
*   What you have said is a common formula trotted out by the police.
*   You needed an arrest to complete your quota.
*   This arrest was a feather in your cap.

Counsel for the Crown should object to comment of this kind as purely prejudicial. It is highly likely that the judge or magistrate will intervene. But this may not always be so. The most effective way to deal with comment is for the witness to appeal to the judge: "Your honour, do I have to answer that question" or "Your honour, I fail to see the relevance of that question".

It is very important that police witnesses, when confronted by offensive comment of this kind do not feel or show concern or distress. Defending counsel is obliged to put all matters which constitute its client's case and which are material to the issues. If they are not put that may lead to the witness being recalled after the defendant has given evidence. If, on the other hand, they are put half-heartedly or apologetically (I am afraid officer I have to put it to you …) that is tantamount to an admission that there is no substance in them. In any case, in the vast majority of cases the evidence of the police upon this subject is preferred to that of the defendant.

## Complaints against police officers

It sometimes happens that a defendant has already lodged a complaint against police. He may seek to justify this by incorporating it into his defence. In other cases the only defence available to the accused is to suggest impropriety by the police. This is frequently so when the prosecution alleges possession by the accused of incriminating items such as drugs, offensive weapons, house-breaking implements and so on. A guilty man has no choice save either to admit that he had them or claim that they were 'planted' on him.

*Always remember that the defendant is on trial, the police are not. Such allegations are generally based solely on the uncorroborated word of the defendant himself.*

Another situation which arises is when the accusations of misconduct by police are not central to the issues in the case. For example, a complaint that the defendant was 'beaten up' at the police station. The only relevance this can have is to call into question the credibility of officers who behave in that way. If the suggestions are denied the accused cannot call evidence in support of them since the matter is only peripheral. The denial by the officer is binding.

## The Magistrates' Court

It is in the Magistrates' Court that the police witness is most likely to encounter the inexperienced or incompetent cross-examiner. It is also in the Magistrates' Court that many cases are based entirely on police evidence so the quality of police testimony is of paramount importance. Typical cases heard in a Magistrates' Court include;

- Vagrancy.
- Living on the earnings of prostitution.
- Unlawful interference with motor vehicles.
- Threatening or insulting behaviour.
- Homosexual offences in a public place.
- The possession and supply of prohibited drugs.
- Assault upon or obstruction of a policeman in the execution of his duty.

The police give evidence of observation followed by arrest, together with any admissions made by the defendant. There will frequently be several officers corroborating each other's evidence. The absence of lay witnesses may well be the subject of comment by the defence, but it is common knowledge that for one reason or another members of the public are reluctant to become 'involved' as witnesses in the less serious type of crime. Criticism of police evidence in these circumstances tends to put them in a 'no win' situation. If they say the same thing it is suggested that they have put their heads together when compiling their notebooks in order to produce a convincingly uniform account. Genuine recollections, it is submitted, could not be so similar. When, however, during the course of cross-examination genuine divergences do emerge these are stressed as indicating the unreliability of the officer's evidence.

In the Magistrates' Court there are many word against word cases - cases in which the court has to decide between two totally conflicting accounts given on the one hand by an uncorroborated police officer and on the other by the defendant unsupported by any other witness. In this situation if the defendant is a convincing witness and of known good character the court has a daunting task in coming to a decision about where the truth lies. *In instances such as this the quality of the officer's evidence must be high to merit a conviction.*

Another factor peculiar to summary trials is that in contested cases evidence of admissions is more frequently oral rather than written. These are commonly termed 'verbals'. These are compromising statements allegedly made by the accused person and noted down by the officer after caution. They are almost invariably attacked by the defence. It may be suggested that no caution was given, although this of itself does not invalidate the evidence. More often than not it is put to the officer that the statement was never made, and that it found its way into the policeman's note-book either because of an error of memory on his part or through deliberate fabrication. It is far more difficult to challenge written statements for the obvious reason that they have been signed in several places by the defendant. To succeed in excluding this form of evidence the defence must raise a doubt as to its authenticity by showing that it was obtained by improper methods or even by downright forgery. Coping with cross-examination on written statements is dealt with in a little more detail further on in this work.

In concluding this chapter, it cannot be stressed too highly that the police officer must possess a thorough knowledge of the extent of police powers. As mentioned earlier in Chapter Three, if you have the law on this subject at your fingertips you will be much more confident when challenged in court by the defence. The foremost powers relate to:

- The power of arrest - with or without warrant; statutory and common law.
- The power of entry, search and seizure.
- The rights of prisoners and suspects - the terms of PACE, the grant of bail from police custody and the rules relating to identification parades.
- Powers of interrogation.
- Police powers relating to public order.
- The procedure for complaints against police.

*Chapter Four*

# Qualities of the Good Cross-examiner

I will now discuss the type of cross-examination a police witness may expect from a skilled advocate, drawing upon examples of the range and manner of questioning police witnesses may be subject to.

## The Blanket Accusation

The clever advocate avoids so far as possible a 'head on' confrontation with the witness. This is because, as every courtroom lawyer knows, witnesses generally harden rather than crack under pressure. In this first example we see how a poor advocate, using a blanket accusation, tends to meet with a blanket denial:

**Example 4.i    The blanket accusation – and denial**

Q:    I put it to you that my client never admitted any involvement in the offence he is charged with?

A:    *He said what I have recorded in my note.*

Q:    Your note is a garbled account of what in fact he told you?

A:    *My note is an accurate record of what he said to me.*

Q:    Your note does not record the whole of what he said?

A:    *My note contains all relevant matters.*

Q:    It contains matters which you considered relevant?

A:    *It contains all matters relevant to the charge which he faces today.*

Q:    Why didn't you write down everything he said to you?

A:    *Because not everything he said was relevant to my enquiries.*

Q:    Was it because you had already decided to charge him?

A:    *I did not think any charge would be preferred except on the completion of his interview.*

Q:      You were the arresting officer?

A:      *The arresting officer, yes. I did not charge the defendant.*

## The 'reasonable' approach

The experienced advocate, however, knows full well that this kind of interrogation of a witness generally gets nowhere. He may therefore adopt the 'sweetly reasonable' approach in the hope of lulling the witness into a sense of false security and so qualifying his evidence in chief to the point where the witness' credibility is undermined. Cross-examination of this kind frequently begins in this way:

**Example 4.ii**    **'Sweetly reasonable'**

Q:    You do understand officer that I am not for a moment suggesting that you are not doing your very best to tell the truth?

A:    *Yes, I understand that.*

Q:    It is not the defence case that you are being dishonest in your evidence?

A:    *I understand.*

Q:    I am merely raising the possibility that you may be mistaken?

A:    *I am not mistaken.*

Q:    I quite understand that that is your honest belief officer, but you would agree that mistakes can be made?

A:    *They can. But not in this case.*

Q:    Yes, officer. As I have already indicated I fully understand what you are saying, but you would surely not claim to be infallible in these matters?

A:    *No. I would not claim that.*

Q:    Since the time of these events have you had a great many other matters to deal with?

A:    *Yes.*

Q:    In some of them your evidence concerned a period of observation similar to this one?

A:    *Yes.*

Q:    Would you not agree that in the course of time memory fades?

A:    *Yes.*

Q:    Particularly when other events intervene.

A:    *I would. But I did make a note.*

Q:    Some hours later?

A:    *Yes.*

Q:    No doubt you have given evidence in court cases very similar to this one?

A:    *That is correct.*

Q:    In some of those cases the defendant has been acquitted?

A:    *Yes.*

Q:    So sometimes your evidence has been mistaken?

A:    *I cannot comment on other cases.*

In this exchange the defence advocate is introducing generalities and inviting the comments of the witness. The purpose is to cast doubt upon the reliability of the officer's evidence. The opposing counsel should object to this line of cross-examining on the grounds of irrelevance. A witness must be careful not to allow himself to be led down this path against his better judgement. It may involve him in serious qualifications of what he knows or believes to be the true circumstances of the case. In the next example we see how the police officer, having made all proper concessions, can reassert what he knows to be true.

**Example 4.iii    Reasserting the truth**

Q:      You say officer that the defendant was immediately behind the victim in the bus queue?

A:      *Yes.*

Q:      And the victim had a carrier bag over her right arm?

A:      *Yes.*

Q:      At the time of the alleged attempted theft had a bus arrived at the stop?

A:      *Yes it had.*

Q:      So the queue was moving forward?

A:      *That is correct.*

Q:      This involved some movement on the part of the persons in the queue?

A:      *Yes.*

Q:      You say the defendant's right hand went towards the carrier bag?

A:      *Yes.*

Q:      A person in a group which moves forward suddenly may raise his hand instinctively to avoid colliding with the person in front of him?

A:      *That may happen.*

Q:      That is a possible explanation of the defendant's actions in this case?

A:      *It is possible. However the movement of his arm was far more consistent with an attempt to steal from the carrier bag.*

In a criminal trial the defence is usually at a disadvantage when the point of cross-examination is reached. The court will have heard the prosecution opening speech and the first witness and already the case may appear strong against the accused person. The task of the defence at this point is to draw the 'sting' from the Crown's case by undermining the evidence so far given. Sometimes prosecuting counsel opens the case too 'high' – a speech which exaggerates the strength of the case for the Crown. This may prove to be an error if witnesses for the prosecution subsequently fail to 'come up to proof', that is to say fail to substantiate the allegations which have been made. A shrewd prosecutor will be cautious in the way he or she outlines the case against the defendant, and does not appear overly self-confident about the evidence which is being called.

The defending advocate on the other hand will not normally make any opening statement, but will save all his points for the closing speech, by which time all the evidence will have been given. It is an important rule of evidence, however, that the defending counsel must put the defence to the prosecution witnesses. Failure to do so will incur the censure of the judge.

Consider a particular instance in a trial of a quite serious charge. When death or injury has been caused by the use of a firearm and the defence case is that the defendant was acting in self-defence or defence of his home:

### Example 4.iv    A serious charge

Q:    The defendant kept the revolver at his home. Is that correct, officer?

A:    *That is correct.*

Q:    Whereabouts was the gun kept?

A:    *In a drawer in the bedroom.*

Q:    The fact that it was kept in the bedroom would indicate that the defendant anticipated the danger that his premises might be broken into at night?

A:    *That is a reasonable inference to draw.*

Q:    Most people are more frightened by the thought of their homes being invaded at night than during the day?

A:    *Yes. I think they are.*

Q:    So, at the time this occurred the defendant was a very frightened man?

A:    *He may well have been.*

Q:    That must be obvious mustn't it officer?

A: *I cannot give evidence about the defendant's state of mind at the time but I would agree that that is likely.*

This is a sensible concession although strictly speaking the officer is being invited to comment on a matter of which he does not have direct knowledge. If, however, a conclusion is an obvious one it may give the appearance of 'stone-walling' for the witness to take the strict evidential point. On the other hand there are times when an officer should decline the invitation to comment. This applies to the state of mind of the defendant. For example in a case of dangerous driving: "You have no reason to believe, officer, that my client was in a hurry?" Answer "I cannot say what his intentions were. I can only say that he was travelling very fast".

### Example 4.v     Questions the witness cannot answer

Q:     My client is an elderly man in poor health?

A:     *That is so.*

Q:     He is 76 years of age?

A:     *That is so.*

Q:     He is a chronic arthritic?

A:     *I understand he is.*

Q:     Do you have medical reports?

A:     *I have.*

Q:     And that is what they say?

A:     *They do.*

Here again this is a situation which the police witness will frequently encounter. Questions may be put of which he or she has no direct knowledge. To give evidence of the contents of a document which the witness has not seen is to invite hearsay evidence. But again it may seem churlish not to agree a commonly accepted fact. If the officer is put in a difficulty the proper course is for prosecuting counsel to intervene and object to the question.

Q:     Would you agree officer that the elderly and infirm feel more vulnerable than other members of the community?

A:     *I would.*

The reason why defending advocates put these sort of generalised questions is to lay the basis for the defence. When the time for speeches arrives these points can be made to the jury with added emphasis because they have already been put to and agreed by the police witness. Thus "You will recall, members of the jury, that when I put this to the officer in the case he agreed with me, speaking as he does from his many years of experience in criminal matters".

Since there are no witnesses to the incident charged save the defendant and, if alive, the victim or victims, the defender will endeavour, within the bounds of relevance and admissibility, to draw from the officer anything which is helpful to his case. This may include the layout of the premises, the time of night when the events took place, anything of relevance found when the police entered the house and matters of that kind. But what actually occurred and whether nor not the actions of the defendant amounted to self-defence in law are clearly matters which cannot properly be put to the officer.

*In a case such as this the officer should in no circumstances be drawn into a discussion as to whether the gun was fired deliberately or went off by accident.*

In the majority of incidents police officers arrive after it has taken place. They are rarely present, particularly in cases of violence, when the alleged crime is committed. Thus, for instance, when there has been a fight involving a degree of violence in a public house the officers are able to give relevant evidence regarding the scene on their arrival. This would include the condition of injured people and the nature of their injuries, broken glass and the general disarray, statements of other persons present and so on. If police evidence is favourable to the accused on any point questions will be directed to emphasising this. But if their evidence is highly prejudicial the defence will run the line: "Of course all this happened before you came on the scene officer". Emphasis will be laid on the fact that police officers have a genuinely difficult task, when arriving in the middle of a disordered situation, in deciding who should be arrested as the aggressor.

The suggestion from the skilled advocate will probably be that the wrong person has been arrested. The type of questioning put to the police witness would be along these lines:

### Example 4.vi   Arriving on scene after the event

Q:      How long was it officer after receiving the call that you arrived at the public house?

A:      *I would say about 15 minutes.*

Q:    By that time the trouble was over?

A:    *People were looking angry but there was no violence going on when we arrived.*

Q:    Nevertheless, it was a pretty chaotic scene?

A:    *Yes.*

Q:    I suppose you quite frequently experience this kind of situation officer?

A:    *Yes. From time to time.*

Q:    And is it difficult to unravel what has happened?

A:    *Sometimes it is not easy.*

Q:    People accuse each other of starting the trouble?

A:    *Sometimes they do.*

Q:    And you have the difficult job of deciding who to believe and who not to believe?

A:    *Yes. That is not always easy.*

Q:    Is there a danger in that kind of situation that you might arrest someone who in fact is an innocent victim rather than the aggressor?

Here the cross-examiner is on dangerous ground. He is putting a hypothesis rather than dealing with the case before the court. The witness should not be led down that road.

A:    *We do not arrest anyone unless we are satisfied that there are grounds for doing so.*

Q:    How can you be sure that such grounds exist?

A:    *We have to act on the basis of our experience.*

Q:    What does that mean?

A:    *We question witnesses at the scene, especially people who were not involved in the incident and therefore are more likely to be impartial.*

Up to this point the cross-examiner can claim to be setting the scene for more particular questions about the case before the court, but he may well expect an intervention from his opponent or from the judge along the lines of "perhaps we could now get to the facts of this case".

Q:    The defendant, whom you arrested, had a cut above his left eye which was bleeding profusely?

A:    *That is right.*

Q:      The victim had a slight bruise on his right cheek?

A:      *Yes.*

Q:      So the alleged attacker was more seriously injured than the supposed victim?

A:      *He was.*

Q:      Did that seem strange to you?

A:      *No. The true test of a situation is not necessarily the extent of the injuries.*

Q:      What is the test?

A:      *The statements of persons present at the time.*

Q:      How many people did you question?

A:      *The victim, the defendant and three others.*

Q:      Who were the three others?

A:      *A friend of the victim and a couple who were having a drink at a nearby table.*

Q:      The friend of the victim could hardly be considered impartial?

A:      *That is correct, but his account was supported by the other two.* (This is a sensible concession, but a properly qualified one.)

Q:      What did the other two tell you had taken place?

This is a risky line for the defence. First of all it lets in hearsay. The officer can answer the question since it has been put in cross-examination, but the defence advocate has no idea what the answer will be. The purpose of the question is to elicit a statement by the witnesses which may conflict with their subsequent evidence, but it goes against the old adage of advocacy: don't ask a question unless you know what the answer will be.

A:      *I was told that there was an argument during which the defendant punched the victim in the face.*

Q:      Yet the defendant sustained the more serious injury?

A:      *There was a struggle during which glasses smashed on the floor. They both fell and I assume that is how the defendant sustained the cut.*

The rule about hearsay must of course be respected by police in the same way as any other witness and any attempt to get round it will incur the censure of the court. But it can be waived by the defence as the above example shows.

## The 'alternative' explanation

Another instance of the 'alternative explanation' type of defence, in a minor type of offence, is found in cases of drivers of taxis and mini-cabs unlawfully plying for hire. Taxis, as is well known, may ply for hire while cruising with the 'for hire' sign on and provided they are not already pre-booked; mini-cabs may not ply for hire at all. They are acting lawfully only when pre-booked for a definite journey.

When mini-cabs are prosecuted for breach of this law there are normally one or other of two defences put forward. The first is that the driver had in fact been pre-booked and mistook the person approached for the client who had made the booking. The second is that it was the plain-clothes officer who, acting in an agent provocateur capacity, approached the driver and requested to be taken on a journey for an agreed fare. This latter situation would remove the element of soliciting on the part of the defendant. Here we have an example of the 'alternative explanation' defence.

### Example 4.vii   The 'alternative' explanation (1)

Q:    Is it correct officer that at the time of the conversation between yourself and the defendant he was parked at the side of the kerb?

A:    *That is correct.*

Q:    There were two of you?

A:    *Yes.*

Q:    Yourself and the lady officer?

A:    *That's right.*

Q:    Neither of you was in uniform?

A:    *That is correct.*

Q:    You were dressed in ordinary civilian attire?

A:    *Yes.*

Q:    He had no reason to suspect you were police officers?

A:    *I am sure he did not.*

This is a 'loose' and unhelpful question from the defence point of view, since the whole case against the defendant is that he did not suspect the true identity of his passengers.

Q:    He will say that it was you who approached him and requested a lift?

Advocates sometimes preface a question with "he will say" or "the defendant will say" although in fact they cannot be certain what any witness will say in the witness box.

A:    *If he says that it will be untrue.*

Q:    When you had the conversation he had not got out of the car?

A:    *He called to us from inside the car.*

Q:    What did he say?

A:    *He said "Would you like a lift?"*

Q:    And your reply?

A:    *We said "Yes". He said "Where to?" We said "Notting Hill, how much?" He said "£10".*

Q:    You were leading him into the offence?

A:    *We were finding out for certain if he was committing the offence.*

Q:    Isn't the truth that you approached him and said: "Can you give us a lift?" and the whole conversation arose from that?

A:    *No. The initiative came from him.*

The above line of questioning takes place in a situation in which there is a sharp dispute on the facts and the questioner has no option but to put it to the police witnesses that his client is giving a truthful account and theirs is untruthful. This will not 'put in' the character of the defendant, since he has no option but to put his case in this way. The attack on police integrity must be more gratuitous to express previous bad character on the part of the defendant so as to assist the court in deciding who to believe. A more subtle defence, in these as in many other types of case, is where the defence accepts most of the police evidence but distinguishes on the mental factor, that is to say the intention of the accused which, it is alleged, has been misunderstood and misconstrued by the police.

An extreme example of this is where a defendant is arrested in the street carrying stolen property and maintains that he found it and was on his way to the police station to hand it in. This may sound particularly convincing when the object of suspicion is a small item such as a purse or a wallet which might easily have been accidentally dropped by its owner. There is a tendency for cross-examination in these cases to invite a good deal of comment by the witnesses which the defence hopes will corroborate the account of the accused. Returning to the mini-cab scenario we see how the defence may build up its case.

## Example 4.viii  The 'alternative' explanation (2)

Q:  The defendant is employed by a mini-cab firm?

A:  *He is.*

Q:  Provided he acts in answer to a booking with his firm he is acting lawfully?

A:  *Yes.*

Q:  In that situation he would not be plying for hire?

A:  *That is correct.*

Q:  He has told you that he was hired to collect two people from Shaftesbury Avenue?

A:  *That is what he says.*

Q:  He says that he was booked to collect a man and a woman?

A:  *That is what he told us.*

Q:  If that is true he was not plying for hire?

A:  *If that is true he was not.*

Q:  You were with a lady officer at the time?

A:  *That is so.*

Q:  You answered the description of the people who had made the booking?

A:  *I do not know if anyone had made a booking. That is what the defendant says.*

Q:  If the booking had been made by a man and a woman you two answered that description?

A:  *If the booking had been made we answered the description to that extent.*

Q:  He told you that he had to pick up two people in Shaftesbury Avenue?

A:  *Shaftesbury Avenue is a big street. He never told us whereabouts he was supposed to collect them.*

Q:  People who book cabs are not always precisely where they say they will be?

A:  *They normally give a clear indication in my experience.*

Here again the witness is being invited to comment. Nevertheless to refuse to comment would leave the suggestion that the defendant had made an honest mistake unanswered. Therefore the reply is justifiable.

Q:     He asked you if you had booked a car?

A:     *No he called out "Do you want a cab?"*

The able cross-examiner always knows that direct confrontation with a witness rarely achieves anything. It is only third-rate advocates who fall into this error. They ask direct questions in a challenging manner which almost always creates an unhelpful hostility on the part of the witness. The skilled advocate has quite a different purpose in mind. His scheme is to remove the 'sting' of the prosecution case and, so far as possible, to create the best possible conditions for his own defence case when the time for that arrives. This tactic requires great subtlety and stealth. It necessitates gaining the confidence of a hostile witness to the extent of extracting at least some concessions and a few qualifications of that witness's evidence.

In many criminal cases defending counsel knows full well that the prospects of convincing the court that the accused is speaking the unvarnished truth are pretty bleak. The reality of the task is to satisfy the jury or the Bench, depending on the type of court, that what the defendant says may be or could be true. A jury must not convict anyone on suspicion which the skilled advocate must create. "Can you go home and sleep comfortably in your beds after convicting this person?" is a well-worn forensic phrase. But before calling his or her own evidence, and before making a final appeal to the tribunal, the defence advocate must do everything possible to blunt the cutting edge of the Crown case. The word I use is 'blunt'. It is only rarely possible to knock out the prosecution attack completely.

## Identification

The area of identification is enormously important, but also extremely complex. As in other aspects of this book, identification is covered in police training, however it is worth considering here as it is often a subject where cross-examination is particularly severe.

The background to the law concerning identification evidence is that it has always been treated with the greatest caution down the years. Although corroboration is still not essential, courts are very hesitant to convict on the uncorroborated identification of a single witness. This is because mistakes are easily made in this area, and have on occasion brought about terrible miscarriages of justice.

One of the worst examples of identification was made during the trial of Oscar Slater in 1909, worth re-telling for its almost farcical nature, if nothing else. Oscar Slater was charged with the murder of an old lady, Miss Marion Gilchrist, in the dining room of her quiet Glasgow house on the night of December 21st 1908. The core of the evidence against him was that of Miss Gilchrist's servant girl, Helen Lambie, who had a very brief glimpse of a man, who was undoubtedly the killer, as he passed her in the hallway prior to going down a staircase and out of the building.

Helen Lambie later made a deposition in New York, where Slater was arrested. This, together with her testimony both in America and Scotland, must be the most extraordinary identification evidence upon which a defendant was ever convicted and sentenced to death.

The deposition read: "I couldn't say whether he had any beard, moustache or whiskers or was clean-shaven; he had a light-coloured overcoat like a fawn colour, about three-quarters length; he wore a cloth hat. I can't tell whether it had a scoop or not. He said nothing but just walked out of the door and downstairs. He passed Mr Adams who was just behind me."

Adams (another neighbour) described the individual as "… not a well-built man, but well-featured and clean shaven, and I cannot exactly swear to his moustache, but if he had any it was very little". He described the man's clothing in general terms and added "I did not notice anything about his way of walking at all". During these extraordinary proceedings Helen Lambie answered questions as follows:

**Example 4.ix    Identification (1)**

Q:    Now will you describe, please, this man that you saw on that night that passed you at the doorway?

A:    *The clothes he had on that night he hasn't got on today, but his face I could not tell.*

Q:    What did you say about his face?

A:    *I couldn't tell his face.* (The witness then gave a brief description of the clothing of the man she saw on the night of the murder).

Q:    Now can you give us anything further in connection with this man that you can tell us about?

A:    *No. I could not*

Q:    Did you notice anything about his walk?

A:    *He was sort of shaking himself a little. I'll show you how he was walking* (illustrating).

Q:    Is that the man in this room?

A:    *I wouldn't like to say.*

Q:    Is the man in this room that passed you in that hallway?

A:    *Yes, Sir.*

Q:    Where is he?

A:    *He is sitting there* (indicating the defendant).

The witness was then cross-examined.

Q:    Didn't you state a moment ago that you did not see the man's face?

A:    *Neither I did; I saw the walk, it was not the face I went by but the walk …*

To identify someone by their 'walk' is a notoriously unreliable form of evidence.

Q:    And all that you remember about the difference in his walk from other men's walk is what you have shown us when you were standing up?

A:    *Yes, Sir.*

This astonishing performance was repeated, if not excelled, at Slater's trial:

*Lambie:*

> *I saw part of his face in Glasgow … Immediately after he passed me and when I turned round just before he went down the stairs.*

Q:    The Commissioner said "What did you say about his face?" And your answer is "I could not tell his face. I never saw his face". How, when you said these things in America and stated on two different occasions that you never saw his face, why do you go back on that now and say that you saw the man's face and recognised him?

Here the cross-examiner was aiming to show that the witness had been 'coached' for the purposes of the trial.

A:    *I did see his face.*

Q:    Why did you say that you did not see it?

A:    *There has been a bit left out.*

Q: Did you say in America that you did see his face?

A: *I do not remember.*

Q: Why do you say that a bit has been left out?

A: *If I did not say it there I could not say it here.*

Q: If you had never seen it in the lobby, why did you say "I could not tell his face, I never saw his face".

A: *I did not see the broad face. He held his head down, and it was only the side of his face.*

Q: But you did not say that?

A: *I know that I can say that.*

Q: You are speaking now after many months – four months and more – since you saw the man in the lobby when your recollection was fresh, on January 26, just a month after the occurrence, and you said that you had never seen his face at all. Can you explain that?

A: *Because he did not look at me, but I saw it when he was going down the stairs.*

Q: Why did you not say so?

A: *I am saying it now.*

Q: Why did you not say it in America when you were asked?

A: (Lambie gave no answer here)

Fortunately Slater was not convicted on the disgraceful evidence of a witness who constantly shifted her ground regardless of the fact that an innocent man's life hung in the balance. Slater was reprieved and ultimately compensated, so far as such a thing is possible. There may have been others who were not so lucky. This thought may be an antidote to the sense of frustration which occurs when a case is dismissed in the face of apparently strong identification evidence.

In the case of *R v Turnbull and Others* (1976) the Court of Appeal gave guidance to judges in those cases where identity is in dispute and the case against the defendant depends wholly or substantially on the correctness of one or more identifications. The matters to which the attention of the jury should be directed include;

* the length of time of the observation,

* the distance of the suspect from the witness at the time of observation,

- the lighting conditions,

- the clarity of the vision of the observer,

- previous knowledge of the suspect by the identifying witness,

- the time lapse between the earlier observation and a subsequent identification and discrepancies of description between the two.

The effect of the Turnbull guidelines is that, while corroboration is not mandatory there is a special need for caution when the prosecution case depends upon evidence of visual identification. The judge's summing up should contain a warning of the need for caution and an explanation as to why caution is needed. The summing up should also deal with circumstances of the identification in the particular case. Moreover, the judge should point out that a convincing witness may nevertheless be mistaken. *This last point is important because there have been classic instances of as many as 20 identity witnesses, all convinced of the authenticity of their testimony, yet all of whom have been proved to be inaccurate.*

The police witness must be fully conversant with the Turnbull Rules since failure to follow the guidelines is likely to result in a conviction being quashed, and will do so if, in the judgement of the Court of Appeal, the verdict is either unsafe or unsatisfactory. Knowledge of the rules also greatly assists the police witness under cross-examination.

**Example 4.x    Identification (2)**

Q:    Did you signal the car to stop officer?

A:    *I did.*

Q:    Are you sure that you gave the correct signal?

A:    *I am quite sure.*

Q:    The car drove past you?

A:    *It drove dangerously close to me.*

Q:    How close?

A:    *A few feet.*

Q:    What do you mean by a few feet?

A:    *About six feet.*

Q:    What about speed?

A:    *The car was travelling fast.*

Q:     How fast?

A:     *About 50 miles an hour. The limit on that road is 30.*

Q:     So you only had a fleeting glimpse of the driver?

A:     *I saw the driver clearly.*

Q:     My question was did you only see the driver for a few seconds?

A:     *Yes.*

Q:     How many were there in the car?

A:     *There were three people as I remember it.*

Q:     But you are not certain?

A:     *No. I am not certain.*

Q:     Where were any passengers?

A:     *One was in the front passenger seat, the other was in the rear seat.*

Q:     Were the passengers men or women?

A:     *All the occupants of the car were men. Young men.*

Q:     I am suggesting that the defendant in this case was not the driver of the car but was in fact the front seat passenger?

A:     *That is not correct.*

Q:     Can you describe the appearance of the driver as compared with his front seat passenger?

A:     *Not in any detail.*

Q:     Because they were both of very similar appearance?

A:     *They were of similar age and general appearance.*

Q:     Can you quote any real point of distinction between the two?

A:     *No.*

Q:     Colour of hair?

A:     *No.*

Q:     Clothing?

A:     *No.*

Q:     Were they both clean shaven?

A:     *As far as I can recall.*

Q:     Then how can you be so certain which of the two was the driver and which the passenger?

A:     *Because I saw the full face of the driver and it was the defendant.*

Q:     I appreciate that is what you maintain officer, but I am exploring the reliability of your identification.

*A:*     *I believe my identification is reliable.*

Q:      I am not questioning your integrity officer, but do you not think that in such a momentary incident you could be mistaken?

*A:*     *I do not think that I am mistaken.*

At this point the cross-examiner is intent upon extracting a concession from the witness that a mistake is possible – even if unlikely. The police witness should not make this concession, firstly because it is comment and not evidence, and secondly because it would undermine the case for the prosecution of which he is a witness.

Q:      Are you familiar with the rules of evidence governing matters of identification?

*A:*     *I am.*

Q:      These rules exist because identification evidence is notoriously unreliable?

*A:*     *That is so as I understand the law.*

Q:      What are these rules officer?

This is an important question since it calls for the officer to give evidence of law rather than fact. It should be strongly objected to by prosecuting counsel. The officer should decline to answer and, if necessary, apply to the court for guidance.

*A:*     *It is not for me to give evidence as to the law.*

Q:      What do the rules say about brief and momentary observation?

Prosecution Counsel:

        It is not for the witness to explain the law to my friend. If he wishes to make a point let him put the question in the context of the facts of this case.

Q:      Do not the guidelines say that brevity of observation is a factor to consider in deciding upon the reliability of identity evidence?

*A:*     *They do.*

Q:      And your view of the two men in the front of the car was very brief indeed?

*A:*     *It was. But I saw the faces of the two very clearly and the defendant was driving.*

When the identity is of another person, for example someone who is with the defendant, Turnbull applies. If the identification is very poor the judge should withdraw the case from the jury. The quality of the evidence in each case will depend on the circumstances and the conditions prevailing. The gravity of the offence in no way helps to substantiate the identification. This author recalls, while on the Bench, dismissing a charge of murder at the committal stage because identity had not been satisfactorily proved. But there may be supporting evidence which strengthens the case against the accused such as another witness or the conduct of the defendant himself.

**Example 4.xi   Identification (3)**

Q:      Whereabouts were you officer, when you heard the shop window break?

A:      *I was in another road around the corner.*

Q:      How far would that have been from the shop in question?

A:      *About 300 yards.*

Q:      What did you do when you heard the smashing of glass?

A:      *I ran towards the place where the noise had come from.*

Q:      What did you see?

A:      *I saw the defendant facing the broken shop window with a brick in his hand.*

Q:      And then?

A:      *I shouted at him to stay where he was.*

Q:      What did he do?

A:      *He looked towards me and then ran away up the road.*

Q:      How far away from him were you when he looked towards you?

A:      *About 150 yards.*

Q:      What was the time?

A:      *1.30 in the early morning.*

Q:      The lighting must have been poor?

A:      *That street is not particularly well lit but there was a streetlamp nearby.*

Q:      You only had a momentary glimpse of his face before he ran?

A:      *Yes.*

Q:      How would you describe his appearance?

A:      *He was clean shaven with short dark hair, height about 5'8" wearing a light coloured shirt and dark trousers.*

Q:      That description could fit thousands of people, officer?

A:  *It fits the person I know to be the defendant.*

Q:  It fits the person you saw in custody at the police station?

## The ID Parade

At this point in the cross-examination the question of confrontation arises. Where the witness confronts the suspect when the suspect is alone, generally at the police station, there are obvious dangers. Nor does the fact that police officers are trained observers in itself eliminate the risk. The suggestive power of an individual, of similar appearance to the suspect, being alone and in custody is strong. Code of Practice D under Section 66 of PACE governs the question of identification out of court. This section deals with confrontation, identity parades and group identification. Paragraphs 2 and 3 of Code D state that an identification parade should be held if identity is in dispute provided that the suspect agrees or unless it is not practicable to hold one in the circumstances. Parades are normally held when the identifier is not a police officer.

**Example 4.xii   ID parades**

Q:  How long after the incident of the shop window was it that you saw the defendant at the police station?

A:  *About two hours.*

Q:  How far from the scene of the incident was it that he was arrested?

A:  *About a mile.*

Q:  Was anything found at the scene to connect this defendant with the offence?

A:  *A brick was found.*

Q:  Where was the brick?

A:  *Among the broken glass.*

Q:  Were any fingerprints found on the brick or anywhere else?

A:  *No.*

Q:  So the answer to my question is that nothing was found at the scene of the crime to connect this defendant with it?

A:  *That is correct.*

This type of question is a forensic stratagem since in such a case it is rare that anything incriminating should be discovered.

Q:  The defendant was arrested as the result of a call on your personal radio?

A:  *Yes.*

Q:  And was the description which you gave on your radio the same as you have given to this court?

A:  *Yes.*

Q:  A description which could fit any one of a thousand people?

A:  *I cannot comment on that.*

Q:  Apart from yourself were there any other witnesses to this incident?

A:  *There was one other.*

Q:  Who was that?

A:  *An elderly man who was passed in the street by the defendant when he was running away.*

Q:  Was he on the same side of the road as the person who you say was the defendant?

A:  *Yes.*

Q:  Was the defendant placed on an identity parade?

A:  *Yes.*

Q:  When?

A:  *Two days later.*

Q:  Why not earlier?

A:  *That was the earliest practicable time when one could be arranged.*

The police witness who arranged or was present at the parade must expect vigorous cross-examination about the procedure, since any breach of Code D may result in the exclusion of the evidence under section 78 of PACE if the consequence of the breach would amount to unfairness or unjust prejudice to the defendant. The rules for identity parades are that nothing must be said beforehand to the witness attending the parade about the identity of the suspect; a witness who has seen a photograph or a description of the suspect must not be shown this before the parade; and the suspect must be placed among eight persons who are similar in age, height, general appearance and position in life to the suspect. To continue with this example;-

Q:  The witness was taken onto the parade?

A:  *He was.*

Q:     He looked carefully at each person on the parade?

A:     *He did.*

Q:     He pointed to someone?

A:     *Yes.*

Q:     Was that this defendant?

A:     *No.*

Q:     He did not identify this defendant?

A:     *He pointed at this defendant after a moment's thought and said "On second thoughts it might have been this one".*

Q:     But he was not sure?

A:     *He was not.*

Q:     On that basis he has been allowed to make a dock identification in this court? His evidence is completely worthless.

A:     *I leave that to the court.*

The rule of dock identifications is that a witness should not be allowed, except in exceptional circumstances, to identify a defendant in court for the first time. Dock identification is unsatisfactory from several points of view.

- Firstly, the lapse of time between the commission of the offence charged and the trial may have been considerable.

- Secondly, the occupant of the dock is separate from other persons in court and therefore conspicuous.

- Thirdly, it is common knowledge that the dock is the place occupied by the accused person.

There can be no objection to a dock identification if at an earlier stage the defendant was pointed out at an identity parade or in less formal circumstances or if he refused the offer of a parade, but generally one of these conditions must apply. Photofits and sketches of a suspect made soon after the sighting are admissible, not to identify the accused but to show the impression which the witness had of the offender soon after the event.

Scientific evidence, such as DNA and fingerprints, is much more difficult for the defence to challenge convincingly. Cross-examination therefore, in a case of contested identity, is generally directed to whether or not the conditions of PACE have been properly complied with when the defendant was under arrest and, if there has been an identity parade, whether or not this has been properly conducted. Questions are likely to be put on the lapse of time before the parade was arranged, the similarity of those on the parade to the defendant, the actions of the witness on the parade and in particular any signs of hesitancy, and matters of that kind.

## Non-compliance with PACE

Cross-examination by the defence is, as I have indicated, frequently directed to non-compliance with PACE. Sometimes, however, the attack on the police may be much more abrasive and suggest grossly improper behaviour. This may be accusations of the use of excessive force in effecting an arrest; bullying and oppressive conduct at the police station; the "planting" of incriminating items on the accused such as drugs, stolen property or an offensive weapon or improper prejudice such as bias over colour and other forms of racism.

These are serious matters which, if substantiated, could have damaging implications for the officers concerned. Such allegations are usually baseless and made as a last resort by offenders who have little else to offer as a defence. However, the defence counsel, if instructed by his or her client to do so, is professionally obliged to put these allegations across.

The counsel is also under a duty to put allegations forcefully and positively, because, if put half-heartedly or hesitantly, the impression will be given that the defending advocate is reluctant to advance his or her client's defence. Police witnesses, whose feelings may be ruffled by these sort of questions do well to remember this. They must also bear in mind that this is always a risky line for the defence since, not only does it frequently expose the defendant to cross-examination by the prosecution on his own previous convictions, but if there is a conviction the ensuing sentence upon a lying defendant who has made injurious accusations against prosecution witnesses will be all the heavier.

Generally speaking these sort of allegations will have a greater chance of a sympathetic reception before a jury than in a Magistrates' Court. Magistrates, particularly in provincial areas, know their local police officers and are in a position to assess the likely veracity of charges of violence and misconduct levelled against them. Juries, particularly these days, may adopt a markedly different approach. They may include members who have no great affection for the police, and if they have read press reports of police officers who have been convicted of criminal conduct they may allow this to affect their judgement in trying the case before them. This is the sort of thing which it is difficult for the judge to put right in the course of his summing up because no judge can discern what is going on in the minds of the members of a jury.

Let us consider a typical example when a 'plant' is alleged:

## Example 4.xiii Allegations of a 'plant'

Q:     You say officer that you arrested the defendant on suspicion that he was carrying an offensive weapon?

A:     *Yes.*

Q:     What gave you cause to believe that he was in possession of such a weapon?

A:     *He was behaving aggressively towards another individual and I thought I saw something glinting in his right hand.*

Q:     What did you think that object was?

A:     *I thought that it might be a knife.*

Q:     What type of knife?

A:     *At that time I was unable to say.*

Q:     So you saw something glinting but could not recognise the object?

A:     *That is correct.*

Q:     It could have been any shiny object?

A:     *In my experience as a police officer an object which glints and which is held in the hand in those circumstances is frequently a knife. It is my duty to enquire further.*

Q:     Did you enquire further.

A:     *I questioned him about the object I had seen in his possession.*

Q:     And what was his response?

A:     *He denied being in possession of any such object.*

Q:     Did you accept his explanation?

A:     *I did not.*

Q:     Why not?

A:     *Because of what I had seen.*

Q:     You may have been mistaken?

A:     *I was not mistaken.*

Q:     Did you search him in the street?

A:     *Yes.*

Q:     And he agreed?

A:     *Yes – somewhat reluctantly.*

Q:     Did you find anything on him in the nature of a knife?

A:     *No. It was a fairly cursory search for the obvious reason that this was in a busy street.*

Q:    But you found nothing?

A:    *That is correct.*

Q:    But you asked him just the same?

A:    *Yes.*

Q:    Why was that, when you found nothing?

A:    *As I have said, it was just a cursory search I carried out and I suspected that he had secreted a knife about his person.*

Q:    Was he searched again at the police station?

A:    *He was.*

Q:    What was the result?

A:    *I found this knife, Exhibit 1.*

Q:    Where was it?

A:    *It was tucked into his right sock.*

Q:    He was in your presence from the time of arrest until your arrival at the police station?

A:    *Yes.*

Q:    Did you at any time see him place the knife in his sock?

A:    *I did not.*

Q:    Can you account for that?

A:    *I cannot. It is something that I missed.*

Q:    I suggest that you missed it officer because it did not happen?

A:    *No.*

Q:    Was the knife listed among his property at the station?

A:    *It was.*

Q:    Did he sign the list of contents as being his?

A:    *He did.*

Q:    Did he sign a list which included the knife?

A:    *No. He refused to sign for the knife.*

Q:    The reason for that, officer, is that the knife was not among his property? In fact you placed it among that property for the first time at the police station?

A:    *That is not correct.*

Q:    I will put it to you bluntly officer: you 'planted' that knife on the defendant at the station.

A:    *That is completely untrue.*

Police witnesses must deal with this kind of questioning in a calm, dignified way. Any sharp response does the witness far more harm than good.

## Cross-examination in particular offences

There is a certain stereotype about the type of defences which police witnesses are met with. An experienced police witness can quickly detect from the way the cross-examination is going which it will be. For example, in offences of assault and assault occasioning actual bodily harm, cross-examination will generally be directed to:

1    **Self-defence.** This must of course be commensurate with the degree of violence suffered or immediately anticipated.

2    **Extreme provocation.** This is rarely, if ever, a defence to a charge of assault but, in jury cases, it is sometimes pleaded on a plea of not guilty in the hope of a 'sympathy verdict' from the jury.

In the case of indecent assault the defence is rarely consent, since unlike a charge of rape it can hardly be alleged that the woman in question was a consenting party. The two most likely defences are:

1    The officer's view was imperfect and therefore cannot be trusted to be accurate.

2    The officer's view was accurate but he mistook what the defendant was doing.

These two defences are clearly only available in the minor types of indecent assault. Where there has been any degree of violence only mistaken identity would seem to negate the charge.

Assault on police, if contested, will be fought on either fact or law or both. If contested on factual grounds there will generally be a blunt denial or an allegation that the officer was using unnecessary force during the arrest or in restraining the defendant and the latter was acting in self-defence. This is the type of charge, however, which may be contested on the law. The defence will then be that the officer was not acting in the course of his or her duty. This will apply if, for any reason, the arrest of an individual or entry into premises was unlawful.

Obstructing a police officer in the execution of his duty is another offence which will be met by the same sort of defence as assault on an officer. A charge for this crime is frequently brought when there has been interference with police activity without actual violence being offered to police. If often happens that when person A is being arrested and person B, a friend, becomes involved on his behalf. Here again the questioning of the police officer concerned may go as to fact, namely that the interference was merely verbal and did not amount to an obstruction or that in law, the officer was not acting in the execution of his duty.

There are many forms of dishonesty punishable by the law. The simple variety, such as theft or attempted theft from the person is generally met by the defence that the police witness misunderstood what he claims to have seen or that an alleged admission by the defendant and recorded in the officer's notebook was in fact never made. In the case of an attempted theft police witnesses may be asked, why the alleged victim is not being called as a witness, how it could be that the defendant did not complete the theft, and why the victim did not appear to be aware that anything was amiss?

Where the charge is that of taking a motor vehicle without the consent of the owner the defence is generally that the defendant did in fact have such consent or has good reason to believe that consent has been or would have been given. On other occasions the plea goes back to one of identification – mistaken identity on the part of the arresting officer as to the driver. (This is usually difficult for the defence to sustain when the particulars taken at the time are those of the defendant.)

In a charge of possession of an offensive weapon the first question is whether or not the weapon is offensive in its own nature. If so, there is very little defence available since the prosecution does not have to establish that it was being carried for an offensive purpose. If the weapon is not offensive *per se* the prosecution must prove the offensive purpose. It is no defence for an offender to claim that he had been the subject of a recent attack and was genuinely in fear that such an assault might be repeated. In such cases the defendant normally pleads that the weapon was an item of equipment used at work and was accidentally on his person at the time, or that he was carrying it to or from his place of employment at the time he was spoken to by the officer.

I have dealt mainly with cross-examination in this work but much of what I have said, particularly in the earlier part, applies equally to examination-in-chief. The important point to remember is that the questions put by prosecution counsel must be carefully followed and concisely answered. The distinction is a technical one, but also very real. Do not at this stage of your evidence concern yourself with what questions might be put in cross-examination. Simply give clear, positive answers to questions.

*Chapter Five*

# Tactics of the Cross-examiner

This chapter focuses on certain regular tactics employed by the defence advocate. One of the most-commonly used techniques of cross-examination is to ask questions to which a very short "Yes" or "No" answer is invited. This method aims to 'pin down' the witness and prevent him from expanding on the answer in a way which might prejudice the defence case. An example of this may be as follows – in a case of driving a motor vehicle without due care and attention:

**Example 5.i    The yes/no questioning**

Q:   Is it correct officer that the defendant was not travelling at an excessive speed?

*A:    Yes.*

Q:   There is no suggestion of that?

*A:    No.*

Q:   You say that he was overtaking on a bend?

*A:    He was.*

Q:   This is not a sharp bend?

*A:    No. It is not.*

Q:   It is, I think, a gradual bend?

*A:    Yes.*

Q:   In the approach to it visibility is fairly clear?

*A:    Yes.*

Q:   He was not flashed by any driver coming from the opposite direction?

*A:    No.*

Q:   You saw no sign of any other driver being inconvenienced?

*A:    No.*

Q:   You heard no sound of any other vehicle applying its brakes?

*A:    I did not.*

Q: If that had happened you would have heard it?

A: *I think I would.*

Q: You are a traffic officer and familiar with those sorts of sounds?

A: *I am.*

Q: You did not hear the defendant being abused or shouted at by any other drivers?

A: *No. I did not.*

Q: That is something you would expect to hear if it had occurred?

A: *Yes. I would.*

Q: The defendant had previously stopped at the lights?

A: *Yes.*

Q: There is no complaint that he 'jumped' the lights or anything of that kind?

A: *No.*

Q: I think your police car followed him for about 10 minutes?

A: *Yes.*

Q: There is no suggestion that he was attempting to avoid you?

A: *No.*

Q: No suggestion of any kind of a chase in this case?

A: *No.*

Q: You say that the defendant was driving in the middle of the road instead of keeping to his nearside?

A: *That is correct.*

Q: Is it also correct that there was a line of parked vehicles on the nearside of the road?

A: *Yes, there was.*

Q: The defendant stopped immediately when you signalled him to do so?

A: *Yes he did.*

Q: In fact he was entirely co-operative throughout?

A: *He was.*

Q: Sometimes, officer, when drivers are stopped and questioned about their driving they can be very difficult to deal with?

A: *Yes.*

Q:      Sometimes they are abusive and even, on occasion, aggressive?

A:      *Yes. They can be.*

Q:      Nothing whatsoever of that kind here?

A:      *No.*

Q:      The defendant was wearing a seat belt as the law requires?

A:      *Yes.*

Q:      He has a clean driving licence?

A:      *He does.*

Q:      Was his car examined?

A:      *It was.*

Q:      Was there anything about its condition which failed to comply with the law?

A:      *There was not.*

The subtlety of this cross-examination consists in two points. Firstly, the questions are framed so as to obtain the answer the questioner requires. The principal thing which a good advocate fears when cross-examining a witness is to be given the wrong answer. Wrong means one which is prejudicial to the defence case. The advocate must therefore conduct the examination of the witness to avoid this so as far as possible. This is done by confining the witness to the precise point – which is by no means always a simple matter. The witness may resent being kept to a 'yes or no' situation and wish to embellish or expand upon his or her answers. If the advocate uses a phrase such as "Please confine yourself to answering my questions" the judge or the opposing counsel may intervene by saying "Please let the witness finish" or words to that effect. If the cross-examiner is allowed to get away with this tactic, the situation can almost be reached in which the witness for the prosecution is turned into a witness for the defence. This the prosecution must not permit to happen.

The police witness put in this position must insist on qualifying or expanding upon the answer given, otherwise a wholly false impression may be given by his evidence. "I would like to add, however ...", "What I feel I ought to say further ..." is an appropriate phraseology for this purpose. If the advocate for the defence tries to shut you up then an appeal to the court is the proper course of action: "Your honour, I think that I should add ...".

The second point to note about the example above is that the cross-examiner has questioned the police witness about various offences with which his client has not been charged. The only charge is one of driving without due care and attention. There is no charge of speeding, failing to stop when required to do so by a police officer, driving without a licence, not wearing a seatbelt or driving a vehicle in a defective condition.

The purpose of this tactic in mentioning these factors is to create a favourable 'environment' for the offender. It is, in effect, a way of putting in the defendant's good character. It is aimed at submitting to the court, indirectly, that a person who has observed the law in all these other ways is unlikely to have committed the alleged offence. Here again the advocate has to tread carefully because he is likely to be asked by the court what the relevance of the questions is. Also, his opponent may object. But generally the cross-examiner will be allowed a certain amount of latitude in this respect. The best course for the police witness is to give short, straightforward answers to the questions unless and until otherwise directed.

The careful counsel always avoids alienating the court. Generally, therefore, the police witness can expect to be treated with a reasonable degree of politeness. There are occasions however when cross-examination can take a pompous or abrasive form. The witness need not be troubled about this because such a method frequently proves more damaging to the questioner than the questioned. The sort of opening gambit one may expect from this type of counsel is:

- "You realise you are under oath officer?"
- "How long have you been a member of the force?"
- "What previous experience have you had of this type of case?"

These sort of generalised and abrasive openings, if not objected to by prosecuting counsel, are normally treated by a court for the irrelevant fatuities which they are. The majority of police witnesses have had at least several years experience. They have also received some years of training. These facts, patiently pointed out to the questioner, provide an adequate and frequently a somewhat deflating reply.

## 'Known' to the police

A suggestion which is sometimes made to the officer is that he arrested the defendant because, for one reason or another, the latter was known to the police and therefore an obvious target for suspicion. Putting this type of defence forward without revealing the full criminal record of the accused can be a delicate operation for defending counsel. Generally it is done where there is nothing to lose in the tactic. The suggestion to the court is basically that yes, the defendant is no angel, but on this particular occasion he was a victim of police prejudice. This is a popular line for defendants to take if they have been arrested for one or other form of soliciting.

**Example 5.ii    Known to the police (1) soliciting**

Q:  You say officer that the defendant was soliciting for the purposes of prostitution?

A:  *That is correct.*

Q:  That is what she appeared to be doing?

A:  *That is what she was doing.*

Q:  Why are you so certain of that?

A:  *She was loitering on the street corner.*

Q:  You mean she was standing there?

A:  *Yes.*

Q:  Is that an offence?

A:  *No, apart from the possible offence of obstructing the free passage of the footway.*

Q:  Is she charged with obstructing the free passage of the footway?

A:  *No. She is not.*

Q:  She is charged with soliciting for prostitution?

A:  *Correct.*

Q:  What evidence is there to support that charge?

A:  *I saw her approach two men.*

Q:  Did she speak to them?

A:  *She spoke to one of them.*

Q:  And the other?

A:  *He ignored her and continued to walk past.*

Q:  Were you able to hear what she said to the other man?

A:  *No.*

Q:  How did he respond?

A:  *He shook his head and walked on.*

Q:  How do you know that she was not asking him the time?

A:      *It did not look like that to me. The man shook his head as if to decline an offer.*

Q:     He may have been indicating that he did not have the time?

A:      *She did not give that explanation when she was arrested.*

Q:     Those are her instructions to me. Did you speak to the men you have referred to?

A:      *No.*

Q:     Why not?

A:      *They clearly did not wish to become involved.*

Q:     So anything she may have said is a matter of speculation?

A:      *Yes – but taken together with the surrounding circumstances.*

Q:     You assumed that she was offering sexual services?

A:      *I felt that was a reasonable assumption in all the circumstances.*

Q:     You knew the defendant as a prostitute?

A:      *I know her to be a common prostitute – yes.*

Q:     You have arrested her before?

A:      *Yes.*

Q:     On the same charge?

A:      *Yes.*

Q:     In the same area?

A:      *Yes.*

Q:     On more than one occasion?

A:      *A number of times.*

Q:     And so, not unnaturally, you presumed she was doing the same thing as on those previous occasions?

It is not unusual for a police witness to be accused by the defence of arresting someone on the basis of a preconceived notion rather than on any solid evidence.

A further example may help to illustrate this in a case where the charge is one of possessing unlawful drugs with intent to supply. A difficulty for the prosecution arises on this charge because although possession is not difficult to prove, the intent to supply sometimes is. I refer here to one individual supplying another or others, not to commercial trafficking. The arresting officer can expect rigorous cross-examination on the subject of intent:

### Example 5.iii    Known to the police (2) supplying drugs

Q:    You understand, officer, that the defendant does not deny being in possession of the drugs. He does deny that it was his intention to supply them to anyone else?

A:    *Yes. I understand that.*

Q:    You understand officer that in order to prove the full offence there must be proof of the requisite intent?

[This is a matter of law and therefore strictly speaking not a matter for the officer.]

A:    *Yes, I do understand that.*

Q:    Where do you say that the evidence of intention lies?

A:    *The defendant was standing on the street corner looking at passers by.*

Q:    Did he speak to any of them?

A:    *No, but he was showing an interest in them.*

Q:    What do you mean by showing an interest?

A:    *He was looking at them closely, and he appeared to be hopeful that they would notice him.*

Q:    What sort of people was he looking at?

A:    *Young people like himself.*

Q:    Did they respond in any way?

A:    *No, but they might have done.*

Q:    Is that an assumption officer?

A:    *I think it is a reasonable assumption.*

Q:    It is not evidence?

A:    *Strictly speaking it is not.*

Q:    When the defendant was arrested was he searched?

A:    *Yes, both on the spot and at the police station.*

Q:    Did he raise any objection to being searched?

A:    No.

Q:    People frequently object to being searched?

A:    *Sometimes they do.*

Q:    He did not?

A:    *No.*

Q:    What did you find on him?

A:      *As stated in my evidence in chief I found five small slips of paper containing a white powder which proved to be amphetamine sulphate.*

Q:      Could he account for that?

A:      *He said that he had obtained them on prescription.*

Q:      Had he in fact obtained them on prescription?

A:      *Yes, he obtained the whole quantity on one prescription.*

Q:      He has been an addict for many years?

A:      *Yes.*

Q:      He has convictions for possession of illegal drugs?

A:      *Yes.*

Q:      He has no convictions for unlawfully supplying drugs?

A:      *That is correct.*

Q:      There is no witness for the prosecution in this case who can say that this defendant supplied or offered to supply them with drugs?

A:      *That is correct.*

Q:      He was of very poor and run down appearance?

A:      *Yes.*

Q:      You arrested the defendant on nothing stronger than suspicion?

A:      *I do not think so.*

Q:      You suspected him of intending to supply?

A:      *Yes.*

Q:      That is suspicion?

A:      *It is reasonable suspicion based on all the surrounding circumstances including the items found on him after arrest. That is why he was charged with this offence.*

The tactics employed by the defence may differ according to the court in which the trial takes place. A judge and jury constitute a very different forum from a bench of lay justices, just as a stipendiary differs markedly from his lay colleagues.

The most difficult tribunal before which to defend in contested cases is probably the stipendiary. This is not because stipendiaries are prosecution-minded. They are not. It is because the stipendiary magistrate has been an advocate himself or herself and consequently is familiar with the stratagems employed by defenders. He has the experience and the authority to intervene if he thinks that the cross-examination is unfair or oppressive or unduly protracted. He also has the requisite knowledge of criminal law and evidence not to be misled by a clever submission or a subtle misinterpretation of the law. He will instantly recognise a false point or an inadmissible question or document. He will not entertain a bad point. There is much less 'elbow room' for the defendant in a stipendiary's court than before a jury. The stratagems which a defender may practice upon a jury could score few points with a 'stipe'. On the other hand, a submission that there is no case to answer, if based on solid grounds, will receive the support of the stipendiary. It is for these reasons that cases before a stipendiary are much more quickly disposed of than those heard by a jury.

## Delaying Tactics

Delaying tactics of all kinds are generally more profitable in the Crown Court than in the Magistrates' Courts. A case which might take three days or more if tried by a judge and jury could occupy only an hour in the court of a stipendiary magistrate. This is partly because although a Crown Court judge has the authority to intervene for the purpose of expediting the case, it is a much more difficult exercise before a jury. Intervention by the judge can be misinterpreted by the jury as revealing a degree of bias and an unnecessary interference by the judge with the functions of advocates.

A further consideration is that in a Crown Court trial the advocates can 'play up' to the jury. It used to be said that the first rule for defending counsel is to 'get into' the jury box. This is particularly so when it comes to speeches at the end of the trial. During my time as a stipendiary magistrate I heard many addresses by defending advocates. Sometimes I found that I was obliged to tell counsel "Please do not address me as though I were a jury." Defenders sometimes endeavour to manipulate and play upon the feelings and sensitivities of a jury. They may, in some instances, attempt to exploit their prejudices. This may all be part of what is called the forensic game, but it can provide an unexpected bonus for the defender. But it is the more protracted nature of the proceedings before a jury that provides the greatest opportunities for an acquittal. The attention of the occupants of the jury box is directed to a variety of matters which may or may not have a significant bearing upon the vital issues in the case. Sifting the wheat from the chaff, that is to say those points which are important from those which are not, may be a difficult task for a jury, particularly a new and inexperienced one. The defender will hope that by such means the 'bull' points for the prosecution become watered down. Prolonged cross-examination of police witnesses may well occur in the course of this scenario.

Consider the case of a violent assault by a man upon his neighbour. Let us further suppose that this attack was the culmination of a long history of animosity between the defendant and his family and the victim and his. It may well be that police had frequently been summoned to the premises to quell previous disturbances. The officer in the case, presuming that he or she has first hand knowledge of the subject, may be subjected to lengthy questioning about this background, either to support a defence of self-defence or to bring out mitigating factors on behalf of the accused. If, as a result of such cross-examination, the jury come to the view that the victim has a history of aggressive conduct towards the defendant or that in the internecine squabbling the family of the injured party has been primarily to blame, this will rebound to the benefit of the defendant.

### Example 5.iv   Shifting the blame

Q:   Are you familiar, officer, with the history of background trouble in this case?

A:   *I am aware that there has been previous trouble between the families involved.*

Q:   What I asked you, officer, is "Are you familiar with the history of that trouble?"

A:   *I know there has been trouble.*

Q:   Do you know the details of the conflicts between the two families? Please be frank, officer.

A:   *I know some of the detail.*

Q:   Have you yourself been called to disturbances between the Smiths and the Joneses? Please don't fence, officer.

Prosecution Counsel:
     Your honour, I object to my friend's comment. The officer is doing his best to answer the questions.

Judge:
     Proceed with your answer, officer.

A:   *I have been sent for by neighbours to deal with disturbances between these two families.*

Q:   How many times and over what period?

Prosecution Counsel:
> Perhaps my friend would ask one question at a time.

Defence Counsel:
> Perhaps my friend would kindly refrain from interrupting.

Judge:
> I think the officer can answer the question as framed.

A: *Twice during the last 12 months I and other officers have been summoned to the defendant's premises over a commotion which has alarmed the neighbours.*

Q: What did you find was going on?

Prosecution Counsel:
> On which occasion?

Q: On both occasions, taking them in order, officer.

A: *The first time was about four months ago when we found Mr Smith and Mr Jones in Mr Smith's garden. There was a furious argument in progress over the noise said to be coming from the house of Mr Smith at night which was disturbing Mr Jones and his family.*

Q: Is it possible to say which of the two was the more threatening and aggressive?

A: *I would say it was evenly balanced.*

Q: Were any blows struck?

A: *No.*

Q: Were the families involved?

A: *They were gathered round shouting at each other.*

Q: When was the second occasion?

A: *About one month ago.*

Q: What were the circumstances?

A: *Similar to the earlier one.*

Q: Where was this taking place?

A: *In Mr Jones' garden.*

Q: Who was involved in the dispute?

A: *As before, Mr Smith and Mr Jones.*

Q: Who appeared to be the more aggressive of the two that time?

A: *I would say that that time Mr Smith seemed the more aggressive of the two.*

Prosecution Counsel:

> Your honour, counsel for the defence is cross-examining about matters and incidents which are no part of the case before the court. What occurred on a previous occasion cannot possibly be relevant to the charge before the court today. The prosecution accepts that there has been a history of trouble prior to these proceedings but would maintain that only the evidence with which the court is concerned today is evidence which bears directly on the offence with which the defendant is charged.

This is a common situation in a criminal case. The defence is attempting to bring in extraneous matters. This may be done in order to divert the attention of the jury from the matter in hand, or in order to provide background to demonstrate a course of conduct on the part of the victim which throws doubt on the victim's account and supports the contention of the defendant that he was acting in self-defence. The prosecution for its part will endeavour to stem this development and keep the case within the confines of the facts which comprise the charge.

Judge: (To defence counsel) What is the relevance of these matters?

Defence Counsel:

> The questions I am putting relate to highly relevant matters. What is alleged in this case is that my client committed a violent act against the victim by knocking him down with a punch in the face and kicking him while he was on the ground. This is denied by the defendant and his witnesses. They say that the other party attacked the defendant and the two fell to the ground. The struggle continued on the ground, and that was the situation when the police arrived. The police chose to accept the victim's version of events and to disbelieve my client. I am entitled to question the officer about previous disputes and prior acts of aggression by the victim against the defendant, in order that the jury may have a clear picture of what led up to the substance of this case and whether the victim is a man on whose word they can rely.

This argument is advanced by the defence, not merely as an answer to the judge's intervention, but for the benefit of the jury also.

Judge: I will allow this line of questioning in so far as it relates to the credit of the victim, but defending counsel must come to the issues in this particular case.

Q: What was the situation when you arrived on this particular day officer? *(and so on ...)*

## Expressing a view

As stated earlier, it is always useful and desirable for a police witness to have a working knowledge of the rules of evidence. If he is asked a question, the answer to which would be inadmissible, the prosecutor, if alert, will raise the objection before the witness has time to reply. But it is infinitely preferable if the witness sees the point first and declines to reply. Otherwise the objection may be made too late or even not made at all, in which case the evidence which ought not to be heard will go in. Basic points of admissibility, such as the hearsay rule, are very important, but so also are the principles relating to the expression of an opinion and the making of comments. The opinion of a witness can only be given in very limited circumstances. An expert, if the court accepts him as such, may give his opinion on a relevant matter, provided that it is not objectionable for some other reason e.g. hearsay. In a criminal trial this will be normally that of a medical or forensic expert, giving an opinion, for example, about the time of death or the likely nature of the implement with which a murder was carried out. Fingerprint experts give their view as to the comparison of the known prints of the defendant and those found at the scene of a crime.

With increasing use of DNA scientific witnesses also deliver this type of testimony in many cases of the more serious variety. By the same token a police officer is entitled to express an opinion as to the speed of a vehicle. This is because his experience in such matters entitles him to be considered an expert. But these categories are restricted and generally speaking an opinion is not evidence. It counts as mere supposition, mere conjecture.

The defence, if they believe that a police witness can express a view which is helpful to their case, may ask a question directed to this purpose and waive the right to object which they otherwise might have.

### Example 5.v    Assault charge

Q:     The defendant is charged with assault in this case?

A:     *That is correct.*

Q:     You would agree officer that the defendant is a small man while the alleged victim is a large one?

A:     *Yes. That is right.*

Q:     The defendant says that he was acting in self-defence?

A:      *I understand that.*

Q:      Is it not rather strange in your view officer that a diminutive man should assault one so much larger?

A:      *Not necessarily, a small man can be strong.*

Q:      In your experience it is normally large men who assault small rather than the other way round?

A:      *I don't think I can comment on that.*

Q:      In your opinion officer, isn't it a somewhat strange thing for a physically insignificant person to attack a powerful one?

Judge:

That is inviting an opinion which does not amount to evidence.

Just as objection can be taken to opinions so also is the case with comment. Comment may amount to the expression of an opinion, in which case it could be objectionable on both grounds, but the real point is that it represents a viewpoint only and is not evidence. Comment often occurs when something is added to what has already been said.

**Example 5.vi    Adding comment (1)**

Q:      Is it correct officer that my client was fully co-operative with police after his arrest?

A:      *That is true. But since he was caught red-handed he did not have much option.*

On the other hand words added which clarify the evidence are not comment in the evidential sense.

**Example 5.vii    Adding comment (2)**

Q:      It is correct that all the goods which my client is alleged to have stolen were recovered?

A:      *They were recovered from the defendant after he had been chased and captured.*

The answer in the second example is acceptable because in accordance with the general principle, the evidential value far outweighs any prejudicial effect.

As with opinion evidence the witness may be invited by defending counsel to comment on a particular matter. If this happens the defence must accept the consequences if the reply is other than was anticipated.

### Example 5.viii 'Putting in' good character

Q:     My client has had a clean record for 10 years?

A:     *For the last 10 years yes – but he has a number of convictions prior to that.*

Here, although previous bad character is not normally relevant, defending counsel has 'put in' character. This is because the defence is not permitted to adduce evidence of part of a defendant's record. It is all or nothing. The police witness is entitled to set the record straight, literally, in order that a false impression of good character should not be created.

*Chapter Six*

# Points of Attack by the Defence

This chapter highlights those areas in which the police witness may anticipate vigorous cross-examination. These concern aspects of police procedure and the rules of evidence therewith associated. It not infrequently happens that the only prospect of an acquittal which a defendant has is to allege that the police have acted unlawfully in the manner of making an arrest; the use of their notebooks; taking a statement at the police station; obtaining a confession; conducting identification procedures; gathering evidence and so on. However, officers who have acted in good faith have nothing to fear from cross-examination on these points, even if they have made the occasional mistake. Most of these issues are covered by the Police and Criminal Evidence Act 1984, but in some instances the common law principles still apply. If the defence is able to obtain the exclusion of evidence on the grounds that to admit it would be unfair to the defendant or that its prejudicial effect would outweigh its probative value or that it is irrelevant or inadmissible on some other ground then the scales of justice may become weighted against the prosecution.

## Confessions

Consider the topic of confessions made to police. This may take the form of oral admissions recorded in an officer's notebook or a more formal confession made at the police station, tape-recorded and transcribed. The latter method, which is now commonly employed, is much harder for the defence advocate to attack if its contents are disputed than was the earlier method of taking the defendant's confession down in the handwriting of the officer.

The essence of the law on this subject is that the confession must be voluntary to be admissible. This was laid down by Lord Sumner in the case of *Ibrahim v The King* (1914): *"No statement of an accused is admissible in evidence against him unless it is shown by the prosecution to have been a voluntary statement, in the sense that it has not been obtained from him either by fear of prejudice or hope of advantage exercised or held out by a person in authority or by oppression".*

If the confession is not voluntary it is not admissible because it may not be reliable as an admission of the facts contained therein. The court must be satisfied that the fear or inducement operated on the mind of the defendant. Examples are where a statement is made by a person in custody following an offer of bail if he confesses to the crime. Ill-treatment by the police is, of course, another ground on which an admission will be invalidated as evidence in court.

Lord Griffiths, in the case of *Lam Chi Ming v R* (1991) defined the principle of the law on the basis that:

1    A man cannot be compelled to incriminate himself and,

2    On the importance in a civilised society which attaches to proper behaviour by police to those in their custody.

In a case, *R v Northam* (1968) the suspect asked a police officer if an offence could be taken into consideration together with other charges at this trial. He was told that it could. The suspect in custody's admission of that offence was subsequently excluded by the court on the ground that it had been made following an inducement.

## The Police and Criminal Evidence Act

The Police and Criminal Evidence Act 1984 Section 76 has embodied in statutory form the law relating to confessions, although the older common law cases are still of important authority. Section 76 states that a court should exclude a confession obtained by oppression or in consequence of anything said or done likely to render a confession unreliable: Section 76 (2). Section 76 (8) defines oppression to include "torture, inhuman and degrading treatment and the use or threat of violence (whether or not it amounts to torture)".

Any form of bullying can amount to oppression. In *R v Paris* (1993) the Court of Appeal held that it was oppressive for police officers to shout at a suspect and tell him what they wanted him to say, after he had denied over 300 times his involvement in an offence. Lord Chief Justice Taylor said in that case that the court was horrified at the way in which the suspect was bullied and that short of physical violence it was hard to conceive of a more hostile and intimidating approach by police officers to a suspect.

There must however be impropriety on the part of the police. The mere fact of the anxiety felt at being in custody does not vitiate a confession. Section 78 of PACE states that the court has a discretion to exclude evidence if it appears that, having regard to all the circumstances including the circumstances in which it was obtained, the admission would have such an unfair effect on the proceedings that the court ought not to admit it. This statutory discretion given to the court somewhat widens the common law position. An inducement relating to something unconnected with the charge will come within the rule. Whether the trial is in a Magistrates' Court or a Crown Court, the burden is upon the prosecution to prove that the confession is a voluntary one. The defendant does not have to establish, even on the balance of probability, that there has been oppression or inducement.

The defence attack on an alleged confession may relate to one of three questions.

1    Was the correct procedure under the Code of Practice in PACE followed?

2    Was there an inducement or some form of oppression of a kind to invalidate the confession?

3    Was there some other factor, such as a language difficulty or mental condition of the defendant which, if the confession were admitted, would render the trial unfair?

### Example 6.i    Confessions (1)

Q:    How long had the defendant been at the police station when he gave you his statement?

A:    *About two hours.*

Q:    Why the delay between his arrival and the taking of the statement?

A:    *There were other matters which had to be attended to.*

Q:    Such as?

A:    *The facts of the offence had to be related to the custody officer, the defendant had to be questioned, searched and his property listed, enquiries had to be made about witnesses and other matters of that kind.*

Q:    Did the defendant complain about being kept in custody for two hours?

A:    *Yes. But the situation was explained to him.*

Q:    Was he placed in a cell?

A:    *Yes. This is normal procedure.*

Q:    Where was he interviewed?

A:    *In the charge room.*

Q:    Who was present?

A:    *Myself and the duty sergeant.*

Q:    Did the defendant have a legal representative with him?

A:    *No.*

Q:    Why not?

A:    *He was given the opportunity to contact his solicitor by telephone but declined to do so.*

Q:    Did you arrange for a legal representative to be present on behalf of the accused?

A:    *No.*

Q:    Why not?

A:    *Because it is not part of our duty.*

Q:    Did you regard the interview with the defendant as an interview under the terms of PACE?

A:    *Yes.*

Q:    Was the defendant cautioned at the outset?

A:    *He was.*

Q:    Of what offence was he suspected?

A:    *Burglary.*

Q:    This is an indictable offence?

A:    *It is.*

Q:    In an interview for that offence the Code of Practice states that a tape-recorder shall be used?

A:    *That is correct.*

Q:    What was the method of interview?

A:    *I put the questions, my colleague wrote down the answers.*

Q:    Why did you not use a tape-recorder? A tape-recorder is more reliable as to what was said?

A:    *The tape-recorder was out of service, otherwise we would've used it.*

Q:    Did you tell the defendant that if he made a clean breast of things he would get off with a lighter sentence?

A:    *I said no such thing. In any event police do not decide sentence. That is for the judge.*

Q:    At the end of the interview did you give the defendant the opportunity to read and sign it?

A:    *Yes.*

Q:    Why is there no signature?

A:    *When it was offered to him he pushed it away and said "I'll take your word for it".*

Sometimes the defence will seek to discredit an alleged confession on the ground that, for one reason or another, the person in custody, due to age, physical or mental illness or an inability to understand the language, was not competent to make the statement and has been taken advantage by the police. The line of questioning may be as follows:

## Example 6.ii    Confessions (2)

Q:    Who conducted the interview at the police station?

A:    *The duty sergeant.*

Q:    He acted on the information which you gave him?

A:    *That is normal procedure.*

Q:    He assumed that the facts which you gave him were correct?

A:    *The facts which I gave him were correct.*

Q:    My client is a foreigner?

A:    *That is so.*

Q:    He is from the Middle East?

A:    *He is from Iran.*

Q:    As an Iranian he does not speak English?

A:    *He speaks quite good English.*

Q:    Would you agree he did not understand much of what was being said to him?

A:    *He appeared to understand perfectly.*

Q:    How long has he been in this country?

A:    *I understand he has been here for three years.*

Q:    Would you expect to speak Iranian well after three years in that country?

A:    *I cannot say since I have never lived in another country.*

Q:     Answer my question please.

A:     *I would expect to be able to speak it to some extent. Different people have varying aptitudes for foreign languages.*

Q:     My client is not an educated Iranian?

A:     *I do not know his educational background.*

Q:     He is a working man?

A:     *He is employed as a labourer.*

Q:     So you would describe him as a working man?

A:     *Yes. He never complained that he did not understand what was being put to him.*

Q:     He was doing his best?

A:     *I cannot answer that.*

Q:     Why didn't you obtain the services of an interpreter?

A:     *We did not consider it to be necessary.*

Q:     Why not?

A:     *As I have said, if a person under interview appears to understand English we do not send for an interpreter.*

The tactics of the cross-examiner here are clear. He cannot put to the officer that the defendant is unable to understand English because that is not so. However, by putting a series of questions on the subject he hopes to implant in the minds of the court the possibility that the defendant did not fully understand what he was consenting to. Counsel is obliged to resort to this stratagem because it knows that the prospect of the police agreeing to the general proposition, namely that the defendant did not mean to say what he has been recorded as saying, is virtually nil.

The defending advocate cannot contradict the case for the Crown. He has to undermine it by building up a 'portfolio' of points adverse to the prosecution which when put together, give the impression of substance. If, for example, the defence at the conclusion of the evidence can point to a number of instances in which the police have failed to comply with the correct procedure, the jury may interpret this as meaning that the police evidence is not to be wholly trusted.

Statements taken down at the police station are clearly more difficult to attack than alleged 'verbals' contained in a notebook and later embodied in a typed document. This is because greater formalities apply to the former than to the latter. Statements by defendants in custody are these days more frequently tape-recorded. Sometimes it may be suggested by the defence that the voice recording does not conform to the transcript, but this is not always easy to establish convincingly. The voices may not always be clear, but if the normal procedure is followed and the defendant is given the opportunity to read the transcript, initial any alterations and sign it at the conclusion, any subsequent attempt at trial to deny the accuracy of the record will not be very convincing. The defendant may of course take the line that he did say what the record contains but the admissions were made for a purpose and do not represent the truth. However, this may lack conviction also.

I have already dealt with the nature of cross-examination of the police witness' notebook. Suffice it to say that this is a more fruitful field for the defender to create a doubt, especially if there has been any failure strictly to comply with PACE.

## Entrapment and the *Agent Provocateur*

It is a principle in English law that, except for inadmissible confessions, illegally obtained evidence may be admitted at the discretion of the judge. Put conversely, there is no rule of law or evidence which says that evidence which has been obtained by improper or unlawful methods must be excluded at the trial provided that its probative value exceeds its prejudicial effect. Nowhere does this question arise in a more important context than that of what is known as 'entrapment'. Entrapment is similar to the method known as *agent provocateur*, although they are not precisely the same. Nevertheless, a scheme of investigation may be covered by both descriptions. The test of the admissibility of evidence obtained by improper means is whether it is relevant or not. For instance;

1      Several young women have been attacked while crossing a particular piece of common land at night. A policewoman, acting as a decoy, walks the same track and is likewise assaulted. Other officers, who have kept their presence concealed, arrive quickly on the scene and the offender is arrested.

2      An employee is suspected of stealing from the till. Marked notes and coins are placed into the till. These are later found to be in the possession of the employee and he is charged with theft.

In both instances a trap has been laid by the police into which the offender has fallen. Both of the methods described above have been approved and admitted in evidence by criminal courts many times.

Lord Fraser in Fox v Chief Constable of Gwent (1985) said: "*The duty of the court is to decide whether the appellant has committed the offence with which he is charged and not to discipline the police for exceeding their powers.*" Yet this doctrine can be carried too far. When the form of entrapment consists of the use of an *agent provocateur* and the subject of the trick is induced to commit an offence which would not otherwise have taken place the court may rule against its admissibility.

Lord Widgery said in *Jeffrey v Black* (1978): "*If the case is such that not only have the police officers entered (premises) without authority but they have been guilty of trickery, or they have misled someone, or they have been oppressive, or they have been unfair, or in other respects they have behaved in a manner which is morally reprehensible, then it is open to the justices (or judge) to apply their discretion and decline to allow the particular evidence to be let in as part of the trial*".

Section 78 (1) of PACE gives statutory effect to the above principle by providing that the court may refuse to allow evidence on which the prosecution proposes to rely to be given if it appears to the court that, having regard to all the circumstances, including the circumstances in which the evidence was obtained, the admission of the evidence would have such an adverse effect on the fairness of the proceedings that the court ought not to admit it. Thus the issue is left to the discretion of the individual judge.

In one well-documented murder case a woman police officer befriended the suspect, resulting in the suspect allegedly making remarks to her about the crime which only the guilty party could have known. The conduct of the police in obtaining this evidence caused the judge to reject it.

Another case in the 1980s followed a large sweep of drug dealers in the West End of London. In that operation the investigating officers pretended to be potential purchasers. This is a perfectly legitimate form of entrapment since it is difficult to get purchasers to give evidence against suppliers and even harder to persuade small time suppliers to name their major dealers. Where the charge is denied the defence is obliged to attack the entrapping evidence as strongly as possible. The discussion between the defence advocate and the police witness in a case such as this could develop along these lines:

**Example 6.iii    Entrapment**

Q:    This was a planned operation to trap suspected suppliers of illegal drugs?

A:    *It was an operation for the purpose of arresting traffickers in drugs in the West End of London.*

Q:    It was a policy of entrapment?

A:    *I do not think the word 'entrapment' is appropriate, the methods employed by police are entirely legitimate.*

Q:    By posing as purchasers you were inducing people to offer drugs for sale and thereby commit criminal offences?

A:    *No. The criminal offences were already taking place. Our job was to investigate them.*

Q:    By acting as *agents provocateurs?*

A:    *No. We were not provoking criminal conduct. This was already taking place. We were carrying out investigations and arrests in the only practical way possible for these sort of offences.*

Q:    Until you spoke to the defendant he had done nothing wrong?

A:    *He had aroused our suspicions.*

Q:    In what way?

A:    *As I said in my evidence in chief, he was standing outside a betting shop attracting the attention of passers-by.*

Q:    What do you mean by 'attracting attention'?

A:    *Looking at them as if inviting conversation.*

Q:    Was there anything else suspicious about his behaviour?

A:    *Yes. On two occasions he stopped young men and spoke to them.*

Q:    What was their response?

A:    *They shook their heads negatively and walked on.*

Q:    He might have been soliciting punters for betting on horses?

A:    *No.*

Q:    Why not?

A:    *Betting shops do not try to attract customers in that way, which in any event would be unlawful.*

Q:    Did you hear what he said to the young men?

A:    *No.*

Q:    So you had no evidence whatever that he was attempting to supply drugs?

A:    *As police officers we were entitled to act upon reasonable suspicion.*

This point may sometimes have to be clarified. An arrest can take place on reasonable suspicion that a crime has been or is being committed or that a breach of the peace is taking place or about to take place. Only if, after arrest, there is sufficient evidence to charge the detainee, will he or she in fact be charged, unless a caution is considered appropriate. Otherwise the arrested person is released.

Q:    You approached him rather than him approaching you?

A:    *We walked past him slowly.*

Q:    So as to attract his attention?

A:    *Yes.*

Q:    To induce him to commit an offence?

A:     *No. It was to investigate whether or not he was committing offences.*

Q:     You spoke to him first?

A:     *No. He spoke to us.*

Q:     What did he say?

A:     *"Anyone in for grass?"*

Q:     What did you understand that to mean?

A:     *He was offering us cannabis.*

Q:     Didn't you in fact speak to him first and say "Have you got any grass?"

A:     *No.*

Q:     What happened then?

A:     *We said "How much?" He replied "£10 a pinch".*

Q:     What did you understand that to mean?

A:     *£10 for each small quantity contained in a slip of paper.*

Q:     What did you reply?

A:     *I said "Give me five".*

Q:     Did he give you any?

A:     *No. He said "Wait here for a moment" and made to go off.*

Q:     And then?

A:     *We arrested him.*

Q:     For what offence?

A:     *Offering to supply illicit drugs.*

Q:     Did you search him on the spot?

A:     *Yes, under our powers of search provided by the Dangerous Drugs Act.*

Q:     Did he object to the search or attempt to obstruct you in any way?

A:     *No.*

Q:     Was anything incriminating found on his person?

A:     *No.*

Q:     Why didn't you wait while he collected the drugs and brought them to you?

A:     *Because we were concerned that he might suspect that we were police officers and abscond.*

Q:     You could have traced him easily enough?

A:     *This was Soho, not Reigate!*

Q:     If he actually had been in possession of cannabis you would have had a cast-iron case?

A:     *That is a matter of comment.*

There are many occasions when the police are obliged to dissemble in order to arrest criminals. Examples of this are when they have to gain access to premises where illegal activity is going on. This may consist of obscene shows, the sale of obscene literature or the sale of alcohol outside permitted hours or without a club licence.

*There is no recognised defence of entrapment known to English law. In the experience of this author, both at the Bar and on the Bench, many corrupt persons have been brought to justice by the secret tape recording of their conversations with fellow conspirators or with detectives posing as such.*

## Observation

There are many cases in which police give evidence involving matters of observation.

The issue in these cases generally relates, not so much to the accuracy of the identification of the accused as to the precise nature of what he is alleged to have been doing. The line of defence is then likely to be along one of two options.

1    It is claimed the observation post occupied by the police officers did not provide them with an unobstructed view or;

2    the actions of the accused were equivocal and at least equally consistent with innocence as with guilt.

If, as frequently happens, the observation position of the police is on the roof of a building it will be suggested by the defending advocate that the angle of vision or the distance involved made the evidence of the defendant's actions unreliable.

If, on the other hand, the observation takes place in a street or a crowded environment cross-examination will be directed to the difficulty of a clear vision of an incident taking place where the view is hindered by the intervening presence of people or vehicles. This line of questioning confronts police witnesses who patrol crowded places, such as the underground railways, for the purpose of arresting pickpockets and persons committing minor sexual offences. It is comparatively easy for an able advocate to create a doubt in the mind of the court, especially since the victims of such offences are generally either unaware of what is taking place or unwilling to give evidence against the offender. Cross-examination in such circumstances may proceed along these lines:

**Example 6.iv    Observation**

Q:    What drew your attention to the defendant?

A:    *Several trains had come and gone but he remained on the platform.*

Q:    Was that sufficient in itself to make you feel suspicious?

A:    *That, together with the fact that he appeared to be taking an interest in women's handbags.*

Q:    What do you mean by "taking interest"?

A:    *Staring at the handbags when the women passed him.*

Q:    Most young women do not carry handbags these days?

A:    *Sometimes they carry shoulder bags. He was looking at those as well.*

Q:    He could have been merely observing the women?

A:    *No. He was looking at their bags.*

Q: Then he boarded a train?

*A:* *Yes.*

Q: And you followed him?

*A:* *Yes.*

Q: Was this the rush hour?

*A:* *No.*

Q: But the compartment was crowded?

*A:* *Yes.*

Q: People were standing?

*A:* *Yes.*

Q: The defendant was also standing up?

*A:* *Yes.*

Q: How far from you and your colleague was he?

*A:* *About 10 feet.*

Q: There were people between you and him?

*A:* *Yes.*

Q: Your view of what he was doing was obscured by those people?

*A:* *No. We saw him lift the flap of the shoulder bag of the woman in front of him.*

Q: I suggest it must have been impossible to see that movement on the part of the defendant in that crush of people.

*A:* *That is what we saw.*

There are some cases in which practically the whole of the evidence consists of police observation. An example of this is a charge of living on the earnings of prostitution. Lengthy police evidence is given relating to the movements of the defendant in relation to the prostitute or prostitutes from whom he is receiving payment. The police keep watch from premises which provide a good view of the area or from within nondescript vehicles. These viewpoints are a very sensitive issue and generally speaking the prosecution is not obliged to reveal them to the defence. If questioned on the matter a police witness should decline to answer and if pressed appeal to the judge for a ruling. In practice the prosecution counsel will normally intervene.

The rule of law protecting police informants from disclosure has been extended to protect the identity of persons who allow their premises to be used for surveillance by the police. The protection also extends to the location of premises used by the police for this purpose.

The reason for this is quite clear – members of the public who co-operate with police must be protected against possible reprisals by criminals. If this were not so they might not give their assistance. Since however it is the prosecution who seeks the protection it must provide a proper evidential basis to support the request, the following principles apply:

1       A police officer of the rank of sergeant or above must have ascertained the willingness of the occupants to the use of their premises and the fact that they fully understand why such use is required, together with any facts which could lead to the identification of the premises and the occupiers.

2       If any change of occupancy has occurred an officer of the rank of Chief Inspector or above must have visited the premises in question and ascertained that the above situation still subsists.

It is for the judge to decide whether, in the interests of justice, the protection should be given. If it is given it is for the judge to explain to the jury the reasons for his ruling.

Another highly sensitive issue for police witnesses relates to confidential communications received from informers. The basic rule is that a witness is not allowed to disclose the identity of his informant or the sources through which he obtained his information. The only exception to this precept is where the judge is of the opinion that it is necessary to disclose the information in order to show the defendant's innocence. The right of the informant to secrecy is not based upon privilege and therefore cannot be waived by the prosecution.

Questions by the defence aimed at eliciting such information should not be asked. If such a question is put the judge should disallow it as soon as it is put. In practice such questions are rarely asked. In any event the answer may prejudice the defence. The principle was laid down by Chief Baron Pollock in *Attorney General v Brant* (1846): *"The rule clearly established and acted on is this, that, in a public prosecution, a witness cannot be asked such questions as will disclose the informer, if he be a third person. This has been a settled rule for 50 years, and although it may seem hard in a particular case, private mischief must give way to public convenience ... and we think the principle of the rule applies to the case where a witness is asked if he himself is the informer".*

The Attorney General's Guidelines (1981) on the disclosure of information by the Crown to the defence exempted information which was sensitive and not in the public interest to disclose it. A typical example would be the identity of an informer, when there are reasons for fearing that disclosure would put him or his family in danger.

*Thus it is important to protect vital sources of information which without that protection might dry up.*

## Standing up to Cross Examination

The credibility and persuasiveness of police evidence is frequently a decisive factor in the outcome of a trial. It is police evidence which covers such crucial aspects of the prosecution case as observation of the defendant when engaged, alone or with others, in the commission of crime, and admissions, oral or written, at the time of arrest. In the Magistrates' Court police witnesses need to perform well because there are many occasions upon which the uncorroborated evidence of the officer is matched against that of an apparently truthful defendant.

The prosecution may be relatively inexperienced in a Magistrates' Court and will have the difficult task of re-establishing the officer's evidence when there has been a severe attack on it by the defence.

In the Crown Court police evidence is subjected to the severest scrutiny of juries – some of whose number may harbour anything but kindly feelings towards members of the police force. It must also be remembered that in trial on indictment the defence, having already received depositions and witness statements, has had ample time in which to prepare its attack upon the prosecution case. Any discrepancy between evidence given in the Magistrates' Court and that put before the jury will be vigorously seized upon.

A further point to note is that the mode of trial in a Crown Court lends itself to stratagems which are not available in summary jurisdiction. For instance, if the admissibility of a confession is challenged in the Crown Court a 'trial within a trial' is held. In the absence of the jury, the police officers responsible for taking the defendant's statement give their evidence and are cross-examined upon it. The judge then decides, after hearing defence submissions, whether or not to admit the statement. If he does decide to admit it, the defence can then challenge its authenticity by the same process in front of the jury. Since, in a Magistrates' Court, the Bench is both judge and jury this procedure is not available. Once again the main principles of giving evidence outlined in Chapter Three, whatever the tribunal, must be emphasised.

The following extract is an excellent example of how the police officer should stand up to cross-examination and is also perfectly illustrates the value of frankness and brevity. The text is taken from the trial of William Joyce for treason in September 1945. Mr G O Slade KC, later Mr Justice Slade, cross-examined Inspector Albert Hunt on the latter's vocal identification of Joyce. Joyce had made a number of broadcasts from Germany during the war on behalf of the Nazi regime which were intended to undermine the confidence of the British people in the prospects of victory.

### Example 6.v    The value of frankness and brevity

Q:    Inspector, I have to challenge your identification of the prisoner's voice on the occasion you referred to in the first months of the war. Do I understand you to say that you have never talked to the prisoner?

A:    *Yes.*

Q:    That was what you said at Bow Street?

A:    *Yes.*

Q:    When the deposition was read over to you, you did not notice that they put down "I have talked to him".

A:    *I do not recall that.*

Q:    What you intended to say, and did say there, as here, was you never had talked to him?

A:    *That is true.*

Q:    Of course the statement that Dover and Folkestone had been destroyed in September or up to October 3, 1939, would have been fantastic?

A:    *Not necessarily. It could have been destroyed.*

Q:    The statement was between September 3 and October 3; that statement was fantastic?

A:    *Well, it was really.*

Here the Inspector is correcting an error. The concession that the claim was absurd should have been made immediately.

Q:    No bomb of any description was dropped in this country until about September 1940?

A:    *I do not know.*

This is the correct answer. Do not accept a suggestion, even from very eminent counsel, unless you know it to be true. If an advocate says "Will you take it from me?" and this is agreed by the witness it amounts to the advocate giving evidence.

Q:     After you left Folkestone on December 10, 1939 you were stationed in London?

A:     *Yes, I have been in this country all the war.*

Q:     Leave out September 1940, do you not know that no bomb was dropped in this country until months after September 1939?

A:     *Well, I can only speak from memory, but I remember the London blitz on September 7, 1940.*

Again, a correct answer. When counsel 'puts' matters to a witness it can be a method of introducing evidence 'by the back door'.

Q:     You were at Folkestone when you heard this broadcast and you say you identified Joyce's as being the voice which used these words? I am suggesting to you that you are mistaken.

A:     *I am not mistaken.*

Q:     To which station did you tune in?

A:     *I do not know. I was just tuning in my receiver round the wavelengths when I heard the voice.*

Q:     Just twiddling it round you heard the voice. Was all that you heard the words "Folkestone and Dover have been destroyed?"

A:     *No. I heard something else but I cannot recall it.*

Q:     Was all that you heard that you can remember that Folkestone and Dover had been destroyed?

A:     *Yes.*

Q:     Was that sufficient at once to discredit in your mind anything that Joyce might thereafter say?

A:     *Yes.* (The witness very wisely ignored the words "at once" and gave a brief and straightforward answer to the question).

The Attorney General then re-examined the witness:

Q:     You said that you had never talked to Joyce. Have you heard him talk?

A:     *Yes. He has got a voice which I would recognise again.*

Q:     Have you any doubt that it was that voice that you heard in September or early October 1939?

A:     *None whatever.*

If you feel that a question is unfair or impossible to answer, appeal to the judge for a ruling:

Q:      Do you not think, officer, that your conduct on this occasion went beyond what is proper professional behaviour by a policeman?

A:      *Your honour, must I comment upon an allegation of misconduct on my own part?*

If required to answer the question a suitable reply would be: "I consider that I acted properly and within my powers."

*Chapter Seven*

# Bail

Than is short final chapter will refer to the terms of the Bail Act 1976 and aims to impart a little extra useful advice on this subject. It is not my purpose to deal at any length with the law. The statutory provisions concerning the granting and refusing of bail should of course been made available to the student police officer during training. Sometimes the officer will be called into the witness box to object to bail, ask for conditions or agree to unconditional bail as the case may be.

Where the offence is not punishable with imprisonment bail shall be granted unless:

1       It appears to the court that, having been previously granted bail in criminal proceedings the defendant has failed to surrender to custody in accordance with his obligations under the grant of bail; and the court believes, in view of that failure, that the defendant, if released on bail (whether subject to conditions or not), would fail to surrender to custody.

2       The defendant need not be granted bail if the court is satisfied that the defendant should be kept in custody for his own protection or, if he is a child or young person, for his own welfare.

3       The defendant need not be granted bail if he is in custody in pursuance of the sentence of a court or of any authority acting under any of the Service Acts.

4       The defendant need not be granted bail if, having been released on bail in or in connection with the proceedings for the offence he has been arrested ... for failing to surrender to custody under a warrant issued by the court of his arrest.

Where the offence is punishable with imprisonment the defendant need not be granted bail if the court is satisfied that there are substantial grounds for believing that the defendant, if released on bail (whether subject to conditions or not), would:

1      Fail to surrender to custody; or

2      Commit an offence while on bail; or

3      Interfere with witnesses or otherwise obstruct the course of justice, whether in relation to himself or any other person.

An officer has to voice his objections to bail if the remand is to be in custody unless this course has already been agreed. An alert and efficient officer will volunteer all the relevant information to the court without waiting for it to be drawn out of him by questions from the court.

Even if there is no application for bail by the defendant, under the terms of the Bail Act 1976 the court has to be satisfied that there are valid reasons for refusal. When objecting to bail, do not merely state this and wait to be questioned by the court as to the reasons. Go straight on to give the grounds of the objection. The information supplied to the court must relate to the particular ground of opposition. For example previous criminal convictions may satisfy the court that the defendant may commit further offences if set at liberty. It would not necessarily be a reason for refusal on the basis that he might not answer bail if he has a good record of surrendering to his bail in the past. Officers are sometimes vague as to which provision of the Bail Act they are citing.

It should always be plain to the court whether or not the police are opposing bail. It is not very satisfactory to draw the court's attention to certain matters and then to "leave it in the hands of the court".

The fact that the offence is a serious one is not in itself a valid reason for denial of bail under the Act. However, the three most common grounds of objection; likelihood of the defendant absconding, committing further offences or interfering with police enquiries cover most of the circumstances behind police opposition.

If bail is opposed because the applicant is already on bail for other offences it is important to know the details of those offences and the dates on which the defendant was previously remanded or committed for trial. The police witness must expect searching cross-examination about his reasons for asking the court to deprive the accused of his liberty. It will look very weak for example if the police contention is that the defendant will interfere with police enquiries if no solid basis for this can be put forward.

As always, be very cautious about replying to the ambiguous questions "would you accept it from me officer … ?" "Is it correct that he has no record of absconding from bail?" Do not accept as correct any suggestion put by counsel unless you know it to be so. Simply say that you do not know or cannot confirm it one way or the other.

Police should check any proffered sureties who are at court. This saves time if the sureties are accepted "subject to police approval". If the police ask for sureties they should be ready to suggest a suitable amount to the court. Finally, police should oppose bail if the offence is grave or the offender has a bad record.

# In Conclusion

I t is not the purpose of this book to criticise the profession of defence Counsel. Provided an advocate does not knowingly mislead the Court, he or she is entitled to exercise skill and guile on behalf of the defendant. A barrister representing the Crown is there to ensure that no unfair advantage is taken of the prosecution witness. The fact is, however, that expert advocacy can, and does, enable many guilty people to escape their just deserts.

The British system of justice is designed to prevent the conviction of innocent. If this results sometimes in the acquittal of the guilty, it is said that this is a price worth paying. This approach is now coming under question. Surely a high detection rate of criminals should be matched by a high conviction rate?

It is not within the scope of this work to discuss the measures effected by government to make a criminal trial less of an 'obstacle race' for the prosecution. One very radical proposal is that the Court should be informed of the previous convictions at the commencement of the case. There is no doubt that such a severe alteration of a basic principle of our law would meet with fierce opposition. This author can see no reason why hardened offenders should be able to hide behind a rule which prevents a jury being aware of their true characters. Be that as it may, I am convinced that it is within the realm of good police evidence that the greater likelihood of the conviction of the guilty lies. If I have made a real contribution in this field I shall have succeeded in my purpose.

# Index

**Agent provocateur** ...............87-92
**Alibi** .....................................................4
**Bail** ...............................................101-3
  opposition to .........................102-3
  reasons for refusing ...........101, 102
  sureties ......................................103
**Cautions** ...............................3, 20-1
**character**
  defendant's previous bad .............15
**Confessions** ...............................81-7
  oppression and ...........................82
  PACE and ...........................82-3, 87
  statements by defendants .........86-7
**Conviction rates** .........................2
**Crime statistics** .......................1-3
**Cross-examination**
  confessions - *see Confessions*
  entrapment - *see Entrapment*
  good ...........................................37-64
  observation - *see Observation*
  particular offences and .............63-4
  standing up to ......................96-100
  tactics .....................................65-80
  *See also Defence advocate, Police as*
   *witnesses, Questioning*
**Defendant**
  acquittal, chances of ....................25
  case against .....................................4
  custody of ..................................22-3
  previous bad character.................15
**Defences** ......................................63-4
  alibi .................................................4
  alternative explanation of ...46-7, 48-9
**Defence advocate**
  aggressive questioning by ..........27-9
  blanket accusation ...................37-8
  comment, adding tactic ...............79
  cross-examination by .............27-33
  defence, written outline of ............4
  delaying tactics........................74-7

disclosure, duty of ....................26-7
ethical principles ..........................26
  disciplinary bodies....................26
good character tactic ...................80
known to the police tactic ......69-74
irrelevant questioning by ........31-33
magistrates' court and ...............33-5
opening statement ...................40-1
opinion tactic............................78-9
reasonable approach..................38-9
role of....................................25-7
weak questioning by....................30
yes/no questioning.................65-69
**Entrapment**................................**87-92**
defence .......................................92
evidence, admissibility of........87-88
PACE and ...................................88
**Evidence**
admissions..................................34-5
admissibility of ...................3, 87-88
confessions .................................81-3
disclosure.......................26-7, 94-6
entrapment and .....................87-88
exclusion ...............................3, 81
hearsay .................................20, 45
identification............................49-57
  corroboration...........................49
  Turnbull guidelines.........52-3, 55
illegally obtained .........................87
in court .....................................5-6
in magistrates' court.................34-5
observation and ........................93-4
of informants ...........................94-6
opinion ....................................78-80
police knowledge of................19-22
scientific ....................................57
*See also Police as witnesses*
**Hearsay**...................................20, 45
**ID parades**.................................57-9
PACE and................................57, 58
See also Identification
**Identification**............................49-57
dock identification ......................59
Turnbull guidelines.............52-3, 55
*See also ID parades*

**Informants** ...............................94-6
**Jury trial** .....................................7
  majority verdicts ........................4-5
  Magistrates' court .....................34-5
  cases heard by.............................34
**Notebooks, use of** .................16-19
**Oath, taking of** ................6-7, 9-10
**Observation** ..............................93-6
**PACE, non-compliance with** .....60-3
**Perjury**.......................................6-7
**Police**
  assault on ................................63-4
  complaints against .............22-3, 33
  morale and ...................................1
  provocation ...............................63
  self-defence................................63
  statutory powers .............19-20, 35
  use of force .................................22
  *See also Police as witnesses*
**Police as witnesses** ............5-6, 9-24
  as effective witness........................24
  assault on police.......................63-4
  audibility..............................10-12
  bail and...................................101-3
  cross-examination of.........21, 27-33
    aggressive response to ...............29
    standing up to...................96-100
  defendant's previous character......15
  evidence in court ........................5-6
  examination-in-chief....................22
  exempted information...................96
  expressing an opinion .............78-80
  first impressions .......................9-10
  hostile attitude ............................21
  impartiality ...........................14-16
  manner of.....................................9
  notebook, use of .....................16-19
    cross-examination and.........17-18
    entries, timing of.................18-19
  oath taking................................9-10
  obstruction.................................64
  offensive questioning of...........32-3
  PACE, non-compliance with....60-3
  presentation of evidence .........10-14
  provocation ................................63
  reasonable grounds to suspect......20

  reasserting the truth .....................40
  rules of evidence ..............19-22, 78
  self-defence................................63
  speech .................................10-14
  terminology.................................16
  Turnbull guidelines............52-3, 55
  verbals................................34-5, 86
  *See also Questioning*
**Questioning**
  adding comment.........................79
  aggressive ...............................27-9
  alternative explanation defence
    ...................................46-7, 48-9
  arriving on scene.......................43-5
  blanket accusation ...................37-8
  confessions and ..............83-5, 85-6
  direct .........................................49
  entrapment and .....................88-92
  evidence-in-chief.........................22
  expressing an opinion ..............78-9
  ID parades ..............................57-9
  identification and ..50-2, 53-5, 56-7
  irrelevant .................................31-3
  known to police tactic.....70-1, 71-3
  notebooks, use of...................17-18
    entries, timing of................18-19
  observation and .......................93-4
  offensive................................32-3, 69
  PACE, non-compliance with....61-3
  particular offences and.............63-4
  police witness standing up to ..98-100
  reasonable approach.................38-9
  reasserting the truth ...................40
  serious charge...........................41-2
  shifting the blame....................75-7
  weak ..........................................30
  witness cannot answer.................42
  yes/no ....................................65-69
**Statistics, criminal** ......................1-3
**Trial by jury** ..................................7
**Trial system** ................................31
  changes to .................................6-8
  professionalisation of .................7-8
**Witnesses**
  alibi ...........................................4
  *See also Police as witnesses*

the **New Police Bookshop**

## The Police Witness: A Guide to Presenting Evidence in Court, by Ronald Bartle

ISBN 1 903639 06 9
Price £9.50 (including postage and packing)

**TO ORDER...**
**Credit card orders** Tel 0117 9555 215 (Brookland Mailing Services).
**Order via the New Police Bookshop Website**
**www.newpolicebookshop.co.uk**
**Payment by cheque** (with order or upon invoice) please direct orders to:
New Police Bookshop, Brookland Mailing Services
Unit 4, Parkway Trading Estate, St Werburghs Road
St Werburghs, Bristol BS2 9PG.
Tel 0117 9555 215 Fax 0117 9541 485
Email npb@brookland-mailing.co.uk
Cheques should be made payable to the New Police Bookshop

**DISCOUNTS...**
**Probationer discounts** - 20% discount for orders placed by probationers
**Bulk discounts** - Standard bulk discounts for book orders in excess of:
one copy - 10%; 10 copies - 20%; 50 copies - 30%

**BULK ORDERS AND OTHER ENQUIRIES...**
email NPBpromotion@aol.com
or write to:
Promotions Manager
New Police Bookshop, PO Box 2
Much Wenlock TF13 6WL

The Police Witness: A Guide to Presenting Evidence in Court, by Ronald Bartle
is published by the New Police Bookshop (Surrey) ISBN 1 903639 06 9 £9.50

## Book titles from the same publisher

A-Z of Cops and Robbers; Contemporary Crime and Police Work -
Terminology Explained, Ashley Rickman ISBN 1 903639 02 6 £12.95

Agricultural Vehicles on the Road: a Guide to the Legislation,
Andrew McMahon ISBN 0 9533058 7 2 £12.50

Child Protection Investigators' Companion, Kevin Smith, ISBN 1 903639 04 2 £13.50

Basic Guide to Forensic Awareness, Martin Gaule, ISBN 1 903639 09 3 £9.50

Crime Patrol: to Recognise and Arrest Criminals
Mike McBride ISBN 0 9533058 1 3 £12.50

Human Rights: The Guide for Police Officers and Support Staff,
Alan Beckley ISBN 1 903639 01 8 £12.50

Human Rights: The Interactive Guide, Alan Beckley. CD version
with update service, licence price according to number of users

Human Rights: The Pocket Guide for Police Officers and Support Staff,
Alan Beckley ISBN 1 903639 00 X £7.50

Human Rights: The Pocket Guide for Public Authorities
Alan Beckley ISBN 1 903639 07 7 £9.50

Investigative Interviewing Explained, Brian Ord and Gary Shaw
ISBN 0 9533058 2 1 £12.50

Known to the Police, Brian Hilliard ISBN 1 903639 03 4 £9.50

The Human Factor: Maximising the Use of Police Informants,
Tim Roberts ISBN 0 9533058 4 8 £14.50

## Journals

Police Research and Management ISSN 1466-7991 £39.50 per annum for 4 issues

Journal of Policing, Ethics and Human Rights £34.50 per annum for 3 issues

## Orders Tel: 0117 9555 215  Fax 0117 9541 485

Email npb@brookland-mailing.co.uk Alternatively write to NPB, Brookland Mailing
Services, Unit 4, Parkway Trading Estate, St Werburghs Road, Bristol BS2 9PG
Cheques should be made payable to the New Police Bookshop. Bulk discounts available

## Enquiries  Tel 01952 728521  Fax 01952 728358

Email: NPBpromotion@aol.com        www.newpolicebookshop.co.uk


## From the New Police Bookshop (E Yorkshire)

Custody Officer's Companion, Stewart Calligan & Paul Harper
ISBN 0 9533058 0 5 £16.50

Points to Prove, Stewart Calligan ISBN 0 9533058 9 9 £13.00

Policing Your Health, Stewart Calligan & Alan Charlesworth (Editors)
ISBN 0 9533058 8 0 £10.00

Taking Statements, Stewart Calligan ISBN 1 903639 05 0 £13.00

## Orders (NPB East Yorkshire titles)

write to Stewart Calligan, the New Police Bookshop (East Yorkshire), PO Box 124
Goole DN14 7FH  Cheques should be made payable to the New Police Bookshop
(10% discount 10+ copies) www.police books.org.uk  email: policebooks@aol.com